GW01150029

Cars for Kids

Editore/Publisher/Editeur/Verleger
Bruno Alfieri

Redazione/Editor/Rédacteur/Redaktion
Bettina Cristiani

Produzione/Production/Production/Produktion
Paolo Sala

Design
Mario Piazza

English translation by Julie Tice
Traduction française par Charles-Marc Laager
Deutsche Übersetzung: Hans Grüning

First published in the United States of America in 1983 by
RIZZOLI INTERNATIONAL PUBLICATIONS, Inc.
712 Fifth Avenue, New York, NY 10019

Copyright © 1982 by Automobilia, Viale Monte Santo 2, Milano, Italy

All rights reserved
No part of this book may be reproduced in any manner whatsoever without permission in writing from
Rizzoli International Publications, Inc.

ISBN: 0-8478-0469-0
LC: 82-42764

Cars for Kids

Edoardo Massucci

RIZZOLI
NEW YORK

L'Autore ringrazia particolarmente il Signor Franco Zampicinini per la preziosa collaborazione, e inoltre: Ugo Donati, Giordani S.p.A., John Knaud, Richard Lines, Giovanni Lurani, Museo dell'Automobile di Torino, Carla Patria, Mike and Sue Richardson.

The Author would like to thank in particular Mr. Franco Zampicinini for his valuable assistance, and also: Ugo Donati, Giordani S.p.A., John Knaud, Richard Lines, Giovanni Lurani, Museo dell'Automobile di Torinó, Carla Patria, Mike et Sue Richardson.

L'Auteur remercie tout particulièrement Monsieur Franco Zampicinini pour sa précieuse collaboration, ainsi que: Ugo Donati, Giordani S.p.A., John Knaud, Richard Lines, Giovanni Lurani, Museo dell'Automobile di Torinó, Carla Patria e Mike e Sue Richardson.

Der Verfasser dank besonders Herrn Franco Zampicinini für seine wertvolle Mitarbeit, und außerdem: Ugo Donati, Giordani S.p.A., John Knaud, Richard Lines, Giovanni Lurani, Museo dell'Automobile di Torino, Carla Patria, Mike und Sue Richardson.

Bibliografia/Bibliography/Bibliographie/Bibliographie

Libri/Books/Livres/Bücher
M. Bossi, *Autohobby*, Priuli e Verlucca Editori, Biella, 1975.
P. Weil, J.R. Chaigné, *Histoire des Jouets Citroën*, Editions Adepte, Paris, 1981.
G. Gardiner, A. Morris, *The price guide to metal toys*, Published by Antique Collectors' Club, Woodbridge, U.K., 1980.
J.J. Schroeder Jr., *Toys, Games & Dolls*, Published by Digest Books, Northfield, U.S.A., 1971.

Riviste/Reviews/Revues/Zeitschriften
L'Enthousiaste, n. 19, Editions E.P.A., Boulogne-Billancourt.
Antique Toy World, Published by Dale Kelley, Chicago.
Quattroruotine, Editore Club Quattroruotine, Milano.

Le bébé auto fotografate appartengono alle collezioni di / The cars for kids which appear in the photographs belong to the collections of / Les autos juniors photographiées font partie des collections de / Die abgebildeten Kinderautos stammen aus den Sammlungen von:
Marco Bossi: p. 52.
Bourton Motor Museum, Gloucs.: p. 39, 64, 67, 68, 87.
Emilio Castellarin: p. 98.
Nigel Dawes: p. 42 (b), 65, 69, 114.
Giuseppe De Matteis: p. 96.
Famiglia Giacosa: p. 40, 66.
James L. Goulding Jr.: p. 86.
Haris Testverek Museum, Budapest: p. 119.
Dale Kelley: p. 74.
John Knaud: p. 24 (a), 58.
Luigi Lazzaroni: p. 72 (a).
Peter Lely: p. 113, 115.
Giovanni Lurani: p. 27, 41, 90 (a, b).
Francis Mortarini: p. 118.
Museo dell'Automobile di Torino: p. 44, 45.
Carla Patria: p. 70, 99.
Franco Sbarro: p. 116, 117, 121 (a).
George Tissen: p. 24 (b), 25 (a, b), 28 (b), 47 (a).

Le fotografie di questo volume sono state fornite da / The photographs for this book were provided by / Les photographies ont été fournies par / Die Fotografien die s Buches stammen von:
Antique Toy World:
p. 24 (b), 25, 28, 30 (b), 31, 32, 34, 35, 36, 37, 47, 50), 51, 53, 56, 60 (b), 76, 80, 83, 86 (b), 97.
Autopresse:
p. 55, 57, 59 (a), 62, 71, 73 (a), 74, 77 (a), 79, 81, 82 86 (a), 93 (b), 94, 102, 103 (a), 105 (a), 106 (a), 107), 108, 109, 110, 112 (b), 118.
Neill Bruce:
p. 39, 42 (b), 46, 52 (b), 61 (a, c), 64, 65, 67, 68, 69, 84 a), 87 (b), 114 (b), 120.
Fuocofisso:
p. 26, 40, 42 (a), 43, 44, 45, 52 (a, b), 63, 66, 74, 84 b), 85, 90 (c), 96, 103 (b), 112 (a), 114 (b).
The National Motor Museum at Beaulieu:
p. 29, 59 (b), 73 (b), 78.

A mia moglie Wanda

UNA PICCOLA STORIA

Sulle imprese dei papà al volante si sono versati fiumi d'inchiostro. Non c'è piega nella storia dell'automobile dove non si sia frugato. Ormai sappiamo tutto di tutti: vita, morte e miracoli.
Sulle imprese dei piccoli automobilisti di ieri e di oggi si è scritto ben poco.
Quel poco non dà che una pallida idea di quanto è stato fatto.
Eppure anch'essi hanno scritto una loro piccola storia.
Una storia innocente e bellissima fatta di milioni di chilometri percorsi quasi tutti a colpi di pedali.
Ben più faticosi, se vogliamo, di quelli macinati premendo semplicemente un acceleratore.
Lo abbiamo scoperto poco per volta scartabellando libri, facendo ricerche, bussando a tante porte.
Nei musei, nelle biblioteche, nelle collezioni e specialmente nelle case, dove la foto del bimbo sull'automobilina a pedali rappresenta il fiore all'occhiello dell'album di famiglia.
Ed è stato come entrare con Alice nel paese delle meraviglie.
Piccoli automobilisti dai visi teneri: ora attoniti, ora raggianti, ora smarriti, ma sempre seriamente compresi nella loro parte.
Una popolazione incredibile di "bébé auto": belle, brutte, ricche, povere, vecchie, nuove, ingenue, sofisticate, arrugginite, tirate a lucido.
E attorno tanti papà, tante mamme a far loro da compiaciuti spettatori.
Valeva la pena di raccogliere assieme tutte queste immagini in un libro. Un libro che rendesse giustizia ai piccoli automobilisti.
Un libro sul quale sociologi, pedagoghi, educatori troveranno probabilmente argomenti di che discettare.
Un libro che racconta una favola moderna. Una favola che comincia così...

C'era una volta un triciclo

Le auto per bambini, come pure i giocattoli in lamiera riproducenti il nuovo mezzo a quattro ruote, fanno la loro comparsa agli inizi del secolo e sono discendenti dirette dell'automobile. Mentre i pionieri del volante cominciano a percorrere, fra il raccapriccio dei contemporanei, le polverose strade del mondo su traballanti caffettiere e alcuni temerari mettono in palio l'osso del collo cimentandosi in spericolate competizioni, qualcuno pensa che sia giusto che anche i bambini prendano parte, a modo loro, a questo eccentrico sport che, nonostante tutto, sta diventando sempre più popolare. L'automobile — non si sa mai — potrebbe anche avere un avvenire. Così nascono le prime vetture a pedali.
Come l'automobile deriva dalla carrozza, così l'auto a pedali trae le sue origini dai velocipedi. I tricicli in ferro, che già esistevano a fine Ottocento, sono la base di partenza delle "bébé auto": vestiti di una rudimentale carrozzeria, corredati di una ruota in più e con qualche opportuno ritocco, si trasformano in piccole automobili per la gioia dei futuri utenti della strada.
Le prime "bébé auto" hanno per lo più un telaio metallico, carrozzeria in legno e ruote a raggi di tipo ciclistico, talora cerchiate in gomma: quanto alla trazione, essa è a pedali con trasmissione a catena come qualsiasi

A BRIEF STORY

Pages and pages have been written about the adventures of grownups and their cars. There's no nook or cranny in the history of the motorcar which hasn't been delved into. We now know everything about everything: inventions, failures and wonders.
However, very little has been written about the adventures of children and cars, past or present. And that little which has been written gives only a vague idea of how much actually has been done.
Finally then, the time has come to tell their story in full.
It's an innocent and beautiful story, made up of thousand of miles, almost all done by pedalling — a lot more tiring, if you like, than those distances covered simply by stepping on an accelerator.
We have found out our information a little at a time, looking through books, doing research and knocking at a lot of doors.
We've been into museums, libraries and private collections, and particularly into houses where photographs of children in pedal cars are the pride of the family album. It has been like going along with Alice into Wonderland.
We have seen young drivers with tender faces, sometimes astonished, other times beaming, sometimes confused, but always seriously playing their part. We have seen an incredible population of "cars for kids", beautiful and ugly, rich and poor, old and new, simple and sophisticated, rusty and shiny. And, around the children and their cars, we have seen a lot of happy mothers and fathers acting as spectators. It was certainly worthwhile collecting all these pictures together into one book which would do justice to these young drivers as well as, no doubt, provide sociologists, teachers and educationalists with material to discuss.
It is a book which tells a modern fairy-story, one which started like this...

Once upon a time there was a tricycle

Cars for children, like the toy reproductions in metal of the new type of four wheeled transport, made their appearance at the beginning of the century and are descended directly from the motorcar.
While, to the horror of their contemporaries, some pioneers at the wheel were starting to travel round the dusty streets of the world in shaky old bangers and some dare-devils were risking their necks in reckless competitions, someone thought it was only right that children too should take part in their own way. After all, despite everything, this eccentric sport was quickly becoming more and more popular, and, you never knew, the motorcar might have some kind of future. In this way, then, the first pedal-cars were created.
In the same way as the motorcar was derived from the carriage, the pedal-car had its origins in the tricycle. Iron tricycles, which already existed at the end of the nineteenth century, were the starting point for our "cars for kids"; dressed up with a simple body, fitted out with an extra wheel, and with a few appropriate small alterations, the tricycle was transformed into a small car for the pleasure of future road users.
The first "cars for kids" had, for the most part, a metal chassis, a wooden body and wheels with spokes as on a bicycle, sometimes with rubber-covered rims. The cars were operated by pedal and block chain, like an

UNE PETITE HISTOIRE

Les entreprises des papas au volant ont déjà fait couler des fleuves d'encre. Tous les plis et replis de l'histoire de l'automobile ont été fouillés et rien ni personne ne reste à découvrir. Mais bien peu de choses ont été écrites sur les aventures des automobilistes en herbe d'hier et d'aujourd'hui.
Et le peu que nous connaissons ne donne qu'un pâle reflet de ce qui a été.
Et pourtant, eux aussi ont une histoire bien à eux.
Une histoire innocente et belle, faite de millions de kilomètres, presque tous parcourus à coups de pédales.
Des kilomètres bien plus fatigants, si l'on veut, que ceux qui ont été dévorés en appuyant simplement sur un accélérateur. Nous l'avons peu à peu découvert en feuilletant des livres, en faisant des recherches, en frappant à de nombreuses portes.
Dans les musées, les bibliothèques, les collections et surtout dans les maisons où la photo de l'enfant au volant de sa voiture à pédales occupe la place d'honneur dans l'album de famille.
C'était comme accompagner Alice au Pays des Merveilles. Tant de petits automobilistes aux visages tendres, tantôt effarés, tantôt rayonnants, tantôt déconcertés, mais toujours profondément pénétrés de leur rôle.
Une incroyable floraison d'autos juniors: belles ou laides, riches ou pauvres, vieilles ou neuves, simples ou sophistiquées, rouillées ou luisantes mais toujours sous l'œil comblé de papa et de maman, dans leur rôle de spectateurs.
Toutes ces photos méritaient d'être recueillies dans un livre. Un livre qui rende justice aux petits automobilistes.
Un livre qui donnera probablement matière à développement aux sociologues, pédagogues et éducateurs.
Un livre enfin qui raconte une fable moderne. Un conte qui commence ainsi...

Il etait une fois un tricycle

Filles de l'automobile, les voitures à pédales, comme tous les jouets en tôle imitant le nouveau moyen de locomotion à quatre roues, font leur apparition au début du siècle. Tandis que les pionniers du volant commencent à sillonner les routes poussiéreuses dans des guimbardes cahotantes, sous les regards effrayés de leurs contemporains, et que les plus téméraires risquent leur vie dans de dangereuses compétitions, d'aucuns pensent qu'il est juste que les enfants prennent part, à leur manière, à ce sport excentrique certes, mais de plus en plus populaire malgré tout. Et puis, sait-on jamais, l'automobile pourrait même avoir un avenir...
Voilà comment naissent les premières voitures à pédales. De même que la voiture à cheval est l'ancêtre de l'automobile, le vélocipède est celui de la voiture à pédales. Les tricycles en fer, qui existaient déjà à la fin du XIXème siècle, sont à l'origine des autos juniors; une carrosserie rudimentaire, une roue supplémentaire et quelques retouches ont transformé le tricycle en une petite voiture pour la plus grande joie des futurs automobilistes. Les premières autos juniors sont le plus souvent formées d'un châssis métallique, d'une carrosserie en bois et de roues à rayons, parfois à bandage de caoutchouc.
Comme n'importe quelle vélo, la traction est à pédales et la transmission

EINE KLEINE GESCHICHTE

Um die Unternehmungen der Väter am Steuer zu beschreiben, sind Ströme von Tinte vergossen worden. Es gibt kein Loch in der Geschichte des Automobils, in dem nicht herumgestöbert worden ist. Von der Geburt bis zum Tode wissen wir alles über alle. Über die Unternehmungen der kleinen Autofahrer von gestern und von heute ist bisher sehr wenig geschrieben worden.
Und dieses Wenige gibt nur eine blasse Vorstellung von dem, was getan worden ist.
Und doch haben auch sie ihre kleine Geschichte geschrieben.
Eine unschuldige und wunderschöne Geschichte, aus Millionen von Kilometern zusammengesetzt, die fast alle mit Hilfe von Tritten auf die Pedale durchfahren wurden.
Sehr viel mühsamer, wenn man so will, als die Kilometer, die durchrast werden, indem man einfach auf ein Gaspedal drückt.
Diese Geschichte haben wir Schritt für Schritt entdeckt, wir haben Bücher durchstöbert, Untersuchungen angestellt, an viele Türen geklopft.
In den Museen, Bibliotheken, Sammlungen haben wir gesucht und besonders in den Wohnungen, wo das Foto mit dem Kind in seinem Autochen das I-Tüpfelchen das Familienalbums darstellt.
Es war, als wären wir mit Alice ins Wunderland eingetreten. Kleine Autofahrer mit zarten Gesichtern: einmal erstaunt, dann strahlend, dann wieder verloren, immer aber ernst in ihrer Rolle.
Eine unglaubliche Anzahl von Kinderautos: schön, häßlich, reich, arm alt, neu, naiv, gekünstelt, verrostet, blankgeputzt.
Und rundherum so viele Papis und Muttis als stolze Betrachter.
Es hat die Mühe gelohnt, alle diese Bilder in einem Buch zu sammeln.
In einem Buch, das den kleinen Autofahrern gerecht wird, das Soziologen, Pädagogen und Erziehern Stoff für ihre Erörterungen liefern wird, das ein modernes Märchen erzählt. Ein Märchen, das so anfängt...

Es war einmal ein Dreirad

Die Kinderautos we auch das Spielzeug, das das vierrädrige Verkehrsmittel in Blech wiedergibt, erscheinen zum ersten Mal zu Beginn unseres Jahrhunderts und sind direkte Nachkommen des Automobils. Während die Pioniere des Steuers auf torkelnden Vehikeln über die staubigen Straßen der Welt zu "rasen" beginnen und ihre Zeitgenossen erschaudern lassen, während einige Tollkühne Hals und Bein aufs Spiel setzen und sich in waghalsige Rennen stürzen, da kommt einem vielleicht die Idee, daß es nur recht und billig ist, daß auch die Kinder auf ihre Weise an diesem exzentrischen Sport, der trotz allem immer volkstümlicher wird, teilnehmen. Das Auto könnte — man weiß ja nie — auch eine Zukunft besitzen. So entstehen die ersten Autos. Wie das Automobil sich aus der Kutsche herleitet, so nimmt das Tretauto seinen Ursprung aus dem Fahrrad. Die eisernen Dreiräder, die schon gegen Ende des 19. Jahrhunderts existierten, sind der Ausgangspunkt des Kinderautos: verkleidet mit einer rudimentären Karosserie, ausgestattet mit einem Rad mehr und einigen zweckdienlichen Verbesserungen, verwandeln sie sich in kleine Automobile, zur Freude der zukünftigen Benützer der Straße. Die ersten Kinderautos haben meistens ein Fahrgestell aus Metall, eine Karosserie aus Holz und Speichenräder vom Fahrradtyp, zuweilen mit Gummireifen: der Antrieb geht mit Pedalen vor sich, und

bicycle, but gradually more and more were produced with a different mechanism which operated on a system of levers, in which movement was transmitted from the pedals to the back wheels.

Luxury toys

At the beginning of the century, therefore, pedal-cars started timidly to make their appearance; a catalogue of 1902 from "Bon Marché" in Paris shows us a wooden car, modelled after a landau, that is, a carriage without horses.
Stylistically, it was perhaps rather outdated; by that time the motorcar had already evolved further than this. Probably people's distrust of the new motorcar and also towards toys representing it told the toy producers not to go too far. All the same, this small landau was a fairly sophisticated toy for the time; it had a wooden body, mudguards, brakes, lights, a steering wheel and a horn. Its cost 65 French francs, a reasonable price for that period.
However, it must be said that even though they were rather unsophisticated, the first pedal-cars were in fact quite expensive and, as such, only within reach of a very restricted number of buyers. The fact is that in the few countries where these cars were made, such as France, they were made by craftsmen and not produced in great numbers, and this explains their price. After all, the same could be said of the motorcar.
In the United States too, pedal-cars were in evidence at the very beginning of the twentieth century: a catalogue of 1903 from "Fair Store" in Chicago shows some pictures of these primitive cars, along with horses, carts and tricycles. Here again the cars were designed like a horseless carriage, and worked in the same way as a bicycle.

Pedal pioneers

It is not easy to ascertain the names of the first pedal-car producers who, as already noted, were sometimes obscure craftsmen. Very often though, it was the manufacturers who were already producing bicycles who put these avant-garde toys onto the market, since they already experts in this line of production and had the necessary tools. A picture postcard of 1905 for example shows us an elegant pedal-car with two children in it; on the back, and advertising caption tells us it is a pedal-car made by "Excelsior", a bicycle trade-mark of the Dutch firm P.J. Wijtenburg that had offices in Middleburg and Vlissingen. For the record, the names of the two learner drivers are also given.
Some cars made in the United States on the other hand cheekily bore on the radiator the names of famous cars such as Cadillac or White but this does not mean that those motorcar manufacturers played any part in their production.
In connection with the names on some of these first cars, let us recall one in particular which crops up quite often in American catalogues of the time: this was the "Hummer" which was a name that characterised rather simple pedal-cars and was clearly written on the side of the cars.

Pedalling faster

The first few years of this century were then rather like a "running in" period; the modest quality of the products, the still limited popularity of the motorcar and people's suspiciousness acted as brakes upon the development of the pedal-car. However, around 1910, the pedal-car started to gain a hold.
In more developed countries, specialised factories grew quickly in number and the models they turned out became more sophisticated and more inviting; the irresistible appeal of children's cars, like that of motorcars, was becoming increasingly apparent as time went by. These "cars for kids" now tried to imitate grown-ups' cars in every aay, and

à chaîne; celle-ci sera cependant progressivement remplacée par un mécanisme à base de leviers transmettant alternativement le mouvement des pédales à l'arbre manivelle des roues arrières.

Un jouet de luxe

Au début du siècle donc, la voiture à pédales fait timidement ses premiers pas, pour ainsi dire. Un catalogue du "Bon Marché" de Paris, datant de 1902, présente une petite auto en bois qui est la reproduction d'un landau.
Son style est peut-être un peu dépassé, l'automobile ayant déjà fait quelques pas de plus. Il est probable que la méfiance engendrée par la nouvelle machine, et par le jouet correspondant, ait poussé les fabricants à ne pas trop se compromettre. Ce petit landau était pourtant un jouet assez raffiné pour l'époque, avec sa carrosserie en bois, ses garde-boues, ses freins, ses lanternes, son volant et sa trompe. Il coûtait 65 Francs ce qui représentait alors, un somme coquette.
Malgré leur simplicité, les premières voitures à pédales étaient assez chères et donc à la portée d'un cercle restreint de privilégiés. Leur prix s'explique du fait que dans les rares pays producteurs, comme la France, ces jouets étaient encore fabriqués de façon artisanale et certes pas en grandes séries. On assistait d'ailleurs au même phénomène pour l'automobile, proprement dite. Aux Etats-Unis, on parlait déjà de voitures à pédales dès le début du siècle. Un catalogue du "Fair Store" de Chicago, datant de 1903, illustre quelques-uns de ces premiers modèles à côté de chevaux à bascule, de petites charrettes et de tricycles. Le style est là encore celui de la voiture à cheval et la mécanique, celle du vélocipède.

Les pionniers de la voiture a pédales

L'identité des premiers fabricants de voitures à pédales, qui étaient parfois d'obscurs artisans, n'est certes pas facile à établir. Ce sont souvent les fabricants de bicyclettes, déjà experts et outillés pour ce genre de production, qui ont commercialisé ce jouet d'avant-garde. Une carte postale de 1905 nous montre, par exemple, deux fillettes à bord d'une élégante voiture à pédales; au verso, une légende publicitaire nous informe qu'il s'agit d'un modèle "Eccelsior", marque de bicyclettes de la Maison hollandaise P.J. Wijtenburg siégeant à Middleburg et à Vlissingen. Pour la petite histoire, les noms des deux automobilistes en herbe sont également mentionnés.
Quelques petites voitures "made in USA" empruntent au contraire avec désinvolture le nom d'autos célèbres, comme Cadillac et White. L'apparition de ces marques sur le radiateur ne signifie pas pour autant que les deux contructeurs aient joué un rôle dans leur genèse.
Et à propos de noms donnés aux modèles du passé, rappelons celui de "Hummer", souvent mentionné dans certains catalogues américains de l'époque; ce nom était toujours bien en vue sur les flancs du modèle et caractérisait des voitures à pédales de conception plutôt simple.

On pedale plus vite

C'est autour de 1910 que commence à s'affirmer la voiture à pédales, après ce que nous appellerons la phase de rodage des premières années du siècle, quand la mauvaise qualité, la popularité limitée de l'engin à quatre roues et la méfiance qu'il éveillait, freinaient encore son développement.
Dans les pays plus industrialisés, on assiste à une prolifération d'ateliers spécialisées; les modèles s'affinent et deviennent de jour en jours plus attrayants. L'auto de l'enfant, comme celle de papa, exerce un charme chaque jour plus irrésistible. Maintenant, les autos juniors veulent être les parfaites imitations de leurs aînées et les fabricants font à qui

wird wie bei jedem Fahrrad durch Ketten auf die Hinterräder übertragen, schrittweise setzt sich aber immer mehr ein anderer Mechanismus durch, der auf einem Hebelsystem beruht, das abwechselnd die Bewegung von den Pedalen auf die Kurbelwelle der Hinterräder überträgt.

Luxusspielzeug

Zu Beginn des Jahrhunderts also beginnt das Tretauto schüchtern uns seine Erstlinge vorzustellen: ein Katalog aus dem Jahre 1902 des "Bon Marché" von Paris zeigt ein Holzautochen, das einen Landauer, d.h. eine Kutsche ohne Pferde, wiedergibt. Vielleicht ist es stilistisch etwas überholt: die Entwicklung des Automobils war schon einige Schritte weitergegangen. Ein gewisses Mißtrauen der Leute dem neuen Wagen und dem Spielzeug gegenüber, das ihn nachahmte, ließ es wahrscheinlich die Hersteller angeraten erscheinen, sich nicht allzusehr vorzuwagen. Dieser kleine Landauer war jedenfalls für seine Zeit ein ziemlich raffiniertes Spielzeug: er besaß eine Holzkarosserie, Kotflügel, eine Bremse, Laterne, Lenkung und Hupe. Er kostete 65 französische Franken, ein ansehnlicher Preis für die damalige Zeit. Wenn sie auch noch etwas roh waren, so waren die ersten Tretautos, um die Wahrheit zu sagen, ziemlich kostspielig und somit nur einem kleinen Kreis von Käufern zugänglich. Es soll allerdings bemerkt werden, daß in den wenigen Ländern, in denen es gebaut wurde, wie eben in Frankreich, dieses Spielzeug noch handwerklich hergestellt wurde, jedenfalls nicht serienmäßig, und das erklärt seinen hohen Preis. Dasselbe Phänomen trat im Grunde auch auf dem Automobilsektor auf. Auch in den Vereinigten Staaten war schon zu Beginn unseres Jahrhunderts von Tretautos die Rede: ein Katalog mit dem Datum 1903 des "Fair Store" aus Chicago stellt uns einige Bilder dieser ersten Autochen zusammen mit Steckenpferdchen, Wagen und Dreirädern vor. Auch hier ist der Stil der von Kutschen ohne Pferde, die Mechanik die der Fahrräder.

Die Pioniere der Pedale

Es ist nicht leicht, die Namen der ersten Hersteller von Tretautos auszumachen, die bisweilen, wie schon gesagt, unbekannte Handwerker sein konnten, sehr oft waren es die erfahrenen und für eine solche Art von Produktion ausgerüsteten Fahrradfabriken selbst, die diese schrittmachenden Spielsachen auf den Markt brachten. Eine illustrierte Postkarte aus dem Jahre 1905 zum Beispiel zeigt uns ein elegantes Tret auto mit zwei kleinen Mädchen an Bord: eine Werbeaufschrift auf der Rückseite informiert uns darüber, daß es sich um ein Tretauto der Firma "Excelsior" handelt, einer Fahrradmarke der holländischen Fabrik P.J. Wijtenburg, die ihren Sitz in Middleburg und Vlissingen hatte. Als interessante Notiz werden auch die Namen der beiden angehenden Autofahrerinnen angeführt.
Einige Kinderautos "made in USA" hingegen tragen auf der Kühlerhaube ganz ungezwungen die Namen berühmter Automobile, wie Cadillac und White; das bedeutet aber nicht, daß die beiden Automobilhersteller bei ihrer Schaffung irgendeine Rolle gespielt hätten.
Und was die Namen der alten Exemplare betrifft, wollen wir besonders einen erwähnen, der in gewissen amerikanischen Katalogen der damaligen Zeit häufiger auftritt: es handelt sich um "Hummer", einen Namen, der Tretautos von eher einfachem Typ kennzeichnete und der auffällig auf die beiden Seitenteile geschrieben war.

Die Pedale werden hurtiger getreten

Nachdem das Tretauto jene Phase der ersten Jahre des Jahrhunderts, die wir Einfahrzeit nennen möchten, überwunden hatte, in der die bescheidene Qualität der Erzeugnisse, die noch beschränkte Popularität des Automobils und das Mißtrauen der Leute eine Bremswirkung

maggiori ed i fabbricanti fanno a gara per introdurvi ogni sorta di accessori e migliorie estetiche: parabrezza inclinabili, parafanghi, targhe, fanali, parti nichelate, paraurti, ruote di scorta, gomme, trombette, sedili imbottiti; il legno lascia sempre più il posto al metallo, le decorazioni ed i colori vivacizzano i modelli che, per la verità, agli inizi erano un po' troppo austeri.

Nasce una piccola industria

Negli Stati Uniti, dove l'industria automobilistica sta facendo passi da gigante, le fabbriche di auto a pedali sono numerose: possiamo citare, fra le altre, la Kirk-Latty, la Toledo, la Gendron, la Sidway, la Pedalmobile, la Steelcraft. I cataloghi americani degli anni che precedono la prima guerra mondiale pullulano di questi nuovi giocattoli: non solo vi compaiono vetturette d'ogni tipo e per tutte le borse, ma anche camioncini, auto dei pompieri e della polizia, furgoncini con piccoli attrezzi da lavoro e c'è perfino un'auto con il suo bravo garage.
Anche l'Europa è ricca di iniziative in questo settore. In Inghilterra, sin dal 1909, si distingue la Lines poi conosciuta come Triang, una marca che, negli anni successivi, produrrà una quantità enorme di splendide vetturette per diverse generazioni di bambini: modelli semplici a buon mercato ed altri di lusso che talora arieggiavano vetture del tempo.
In Italia la Giordani, fabbrica di carrozzine da passeggio, tricicli e giocattoli per bimbi, le cui origini risalgono al 1895, ci mostra in un catalogo del 1915 uno dei suoi primi modelli: una "automobile a pedali" in versione ad uno o due posti; la linea è piuttosto essenziale, la trasmissione è a catena, il cofano ricorda quello di una Renault, le ruote sono a raggi e, se rivestite in gomma, comportano un aumento del prezzo di circa un quarto: da 40 lire si passa ad oltre 50. Gli *optionals* erano già cari.
In Francia, patria di mille imprese automobilistiche e, come abbiamo visto, all'avanguardia nella produzione di questi nuovi giocattoli, si perfezionano i modelli e si adeguano alle nuove esigenze del mercato. Un catalogo del 1914, ancora del "Bon Marché", annuncia una novità consistente in una vetturetta a due posti che assomiglia ad una Peugeot Grand Prix 1911 ed ha la pedaliera montata su cuscinetti a sfere. Di questa Peugeot in miniatura il costruttore offre più versioni di prezzo differente a seconda delle dimensioni e dei dettagli: la più cara, lunga circa 2 metri, costa 175 franchi, la più economica 25.

Variazioni sul tema

Abbiamo fin qui parlato di trazione a pedali: vogliamo ricordare anche un altro sistema di locomozione che, rifacendosi un po' al canottaggio, venne sperimentato a quell'epoca, ma con limitato successo.
Ne troviamo notizia, per esempio, in una inserzione pubblicitaria della Winkel di Batavia, in cui veniva reclamizzato un veicolo per bambini chiamato "Vliegende Hollander" ovvero "l'olandese volante", mosso con la forza delle braccia anzichè delle gambe. Per la verità, questo veicolo per bambini aveva ben poco in comune con l'automobile, se non le quattro ruote.
Pure in Inghilterra fu messo in commercio questa specie di "kart" privo di carrozzeria e azionato a braccia; si chiamava "Empire Racer" e lo troviamo anche nei cataloghi degli Stati Uniti: era conosciuto come "Hand car" o anche "Irish Mail". Probabilmente non incontrò grandi simpatie perché appagava poco l'occhio.
Un altro curioso sistema di trazione è quello che si vede in un catalogo degli anni venti della fabbrica tedesca Kohnstam, nota anche come "Moko". Tra gli altri modelli a pedali con trasmissione a leve o a catena compare infatti una vetturetta azionata da due manovelle piuttosto antiestetiche poste sul cofano.

manufacturers competed to introduce every type of accessory and show the best styling.
So cars were provided with sloping windscreens, mudguards, number plates, lights, nickel-plated parts, bumpers, spare wheels, tyres, horns, padded seats; wood was replaced more and more often by metal and colour and decorations brightened up the models, which to be frank, had at first been rather too austere in appearance.

Birth of a small industry

In the United States, where the motorcar industry was taking giant steps forward, pedal-car factories were numerous; we can name, among others, Kirk-Latty, Toledo, Gendron, Sidway, Pedalmobile, and Steelcraft. American catalogues which came out in the years preceding the first world war were full of these new toys; not only did model cars appear of every type and for every purse, but also model lorries, fire-engines and police cars, vans with small work accessories and even a car with its own little garage.
Europe too was full of enterprise in this field. In England a company called "Lines", later known as "Triang", started to make its mark around 1909. It was a trademark which in the following years produced a huge number of splendid model cars for several generations of children: some were simple, good value models, others luxury models which now and then closely resembled the motorcars of the day.
In Italy Giordani, founded in 1895 and manufacturers of push-chairs, tricycles and childrens toys, show us in a catalogue of 1915 one of their first models: a "pedal car" in versions with one or two seats. The line was rather basic, with block chain traction, a bonnet reminiscent of a Renault, and wheels with spokes. If tyres were provided too, then the car went up about a quarter in price; from 40 lire it went up to over 50 lire. "Optionals" were already expensive.
France, where a lot was happening in the car world, was, as we have seen, already in the lead in the production of these new toys, and now models were being perfected and brought into line with the new demands of the market.
A catalogue of 1914, again from "Bon Marché", announces a real novelty: a two-seater car which looked like a Peugeot Grand Prix 1911 and which had the pedals mounted on ball-bearings. The manufacturer offered different versions of this miniature Peugeot at various prices, the price depending on the size and the details. The most expensive was about 2 metres in length cost 175 French francs, while the cheapest cost 25 francs.

Variations on the theme

Up to this point we have talked only of pedal traction. We should however say now that there was another system of locomotion which bore some similarity to rowing and was experimented with though with limited success.
We find mention of it for example in an advertisement for Winkel of Batavia, in which a vehicle for children called the "Vliegende Hollander", (the "Flying Dutchman") was advertised. It was operated by using the arms as well as the legs, and in fact had very little to do with the motorcar except the four wheels.
In England too this type of go-kart, without a bodywork and operated by the arms, was put on the market. It was called the "Empire Racer", and we also come across it in catalogues from the United States; it was known there as the "Hand car" or the "Irish Mail". It probably did not meet with great favour as it was not very appealing to look at.
Another strange system of traction was one which appeared in a catalogue in the 1920s from the German manufacturers Kohnstam, also

ajoutera le plus d'accessoires et créera la ligne la plus esthétique: pare-brises rabattables, garde-boues, plaques d'immatriculation, phares, parties nickelées, pare-chocs, roues de secours, pneus, trompes, sièges rembourrés.
Le bois cède peu à peu la place au métal, tandis que décorations et couleurs ravivent les modèles qui étaient, il est vrai, encore trop austères.

La naissance d'une petite industrie

Aux Etats Unis, où l'industrie automobile progresse à pas de géants, les ateliers de voitures à pédales se multiplient: citons, entre autres, Kirk-Latty, Toledo, Gendron, Sidway Pedalmobile et Steelcraft. Avant la première guerre mondiale, ces nouveaux jouets envahissent les catalogues américains. On y rencontre non seulement toutes sortes de petites voitures pour toutes les bourses, mais encore des camions, des voitures de pompiers et de police, des fourgons avec leur outils de travail et même un voiture avec son garage.
Les initiatives fleurissent en Europe aussi.
En Angleterre, Lines (la future Triang) se distingue dès 1909 en produisant une quantité impressionante de splendides petites voitures pour plusieurs générations d'enfants: des modèles simples et bon marché à côté de modèles de luxe qui imitaient parfois les automobiles de l'époque.
En Italie, la Maison Giordani fondée en 1895 pour la production de poussettes, de tricycles et de jouets en général, propose un de ses premiers modèles dans un catalogue de 1915: une "automobile à pédales" à une ou deux places, de ligne plutôt sobre avec un capot rappelant celui d'une Renault, une chaîne de transmission et des roues à rayons; son prix augmente d'un quart environ avec des roues à bandage de caoutchouc (de 40 lires à plus de 50 lires). Les accessoires en option étaient déjà chers.
En France, patrie de nombreux constructeurs automobiles et, nous l'avons vu, à l'avant-garde dans la production de ces nouveaux jouets, les modèles se perfectionnent et se conforment aux nouvelles exigences du marché. Un catalogue de 1914, toujours du "Bon Marché", annonce une nouveauté: une petite voiture à deux places qui ressemble à une Peugeot Grand Prix 1911, avec pédalier monté sur roulements à billes. Cette Peugeot miniature existe en plusieurs versions, plus ou moins coûteuses en fonction de ses dimensions et de sa finition: la plus chère, mesurant environ 2 mètres, coûte 175 francs, et la plus économique, 25 francs.

Quelques variations sur le thème

Nous avons jusqu'ici parlé de traction à pédales, mais nous devons mentionner un autre système de locomotion, inspiré du canotage et qui fut expérimenté à l'époque sans néanmoins obtenir un grand succès. On le retrouve, par exemple, dans une annonce publicitaire de la Maison Winkel des Pays-Bas qui présentait un véhicule pour enfants appelé "Vliegende Hollander", soit "le hollandais volant", mû par la force des bras et non par celle des jambes. Il est vrai que ce véhicule avait bien peu de choses en commun avec l'automobile, à part les quatre roues.
Cette espèce de "kart" sans carrosserie, actionné par la force des bras, a également été commercialisé en Angleterre sous le nom d'"Empire Racer" et aux Etats Unis où il était appelé "Hand car" ou "Irish Mail". Il est probable que le manque d'enthousiasme à son égard soit dû à son apparence peu flatteuse.
Un autre système de traction, tout aussi curieux, est illustré dans un catalogue des années vingt de la Maison allemande Kohnstam, plus connue sous le nom de "Moko". Parmi les modèles à pédales avec transmission à leviers ou à chaîne, figure en effet un petite voiture

hatten, beginnt es sich um das Jahr 1910 durchzusetzen. In den industriell entwickelteren Ländern vermehren sich die auf seine Herstellung spezialisierten Fabriken, die Modelle verfeinern sich und werden immer einladender. Das Kinderauto, wie das größere Papas, läßt seinen unwiderstehlichen Zauber von Tag zu Tag mehr verspüren. Die Kinderautos versuchen nun in allem und jedem dem größeren Brüder nachzuahmen, und die Hersteller versuchen um die Wette, jede Art von Zubehör und ästhetischen Verbesserungen anzubringen: neigbare Windschutzscheiben, Kotflügel, Nummernschilder, Scheinwerfer, Vernikkelungen, Stoßstangen, Ersatzräder, Reifen, Hupen, gepolsterte Sitze; das Holz weicht immer mehr dem Metall, die Verzierungen und Farben geben den Modellen ein lebhafteres Aussehen, die, um die Wahrheit zu sagen, zu Beginn etwas zu streng gewesen waren.

Es entsteht eine kleine Industrie

In den Vereinigten Staaten, wo die Automobilindustrie mit Riesenschritten fortschreitet, gibt es zahlreiche Tretautofabriken: wir können unter anderen anführen: Kirk-Latty, Toledo, Gendron, Sidway, Pedalmobile, Steelcraft. Die Kataloge dieser Jahre vor dem ersten Weltkrieg wimmeln von diesem neuen Spielzeug: nicht nur Autos von jedem Typ und für jede Geldbörse sind zu sehen, nein, auch kleine Lastwagen, Feuerwehr-und Polizeiautos, Lieferwagen mit kleinen Arbeitsgeräten und schließlich sogar ein Auto mit seiner Garage.
Auch Europa ist reich an Initiativen auf diesem Sektor. In England zeichnet sich seit 1909 die Marke Lines, später unter der Bezeichnung Triang bekannt, aus, die in den darauffolgenden Jahren eine ungeheure Menge von wunderschönen kleinen Autos für verschiedene Kindergenerationen herstellen sollte: einfache preiswerte sowie Luxusmodelle, die manchmal den großen Wagen der damaligen Zeit ähnelten. In Italien zeigt die Firma Giordani, die Kinderwagen, Dreiräder und Spielzeug herstellt und die 1895 gegründet wurde, in einem Katalog von 1915 eines ihrer ersten Modelle: ein "Automobil mit Pedalen", ein- oder zweisitzig; die Linie beschränkt sich auf das Wesentliche, die Übertragung geht durch eine Kette vor sich, die Motorhaube erinnert an die eines Renaults, die Speichenräder erhöhen den Preis, wenn sie auf Gummi laufen, um ungefähr ein Viertel: von 40 Lire auf über 50. Schon damals kosteten die Extras viel.
In Frankreich, der Heimat der tausend Automobilfabriken, und, wie wir gesehen haben, in der Herstellung dieses neuen Spielzeugs den anderen weit voraus, werden die Modelle vervollkommnet und den neuen Erfordernissen des Marktes angepaßt. Ein Katalog von 1914, ebenfalls des "Bon Marché", kündigt eine Neuigkeit an, die in einem zweisitzigen Autochen besteht, das einem Peugeot Grand Prix 1911 ähnelt und ein kugelgelagertes Pedalwerk aufweist. Von diesem Miniaturpeugeot bietet der Hersteller verschiedene Versionen in verschiedenen Preislagen an, je nach Ausmaßen und Ausstattung: das teuerste, ungefähr zwei Meter lange Modell kostet 175 Franken, das billigste 25.

Variationen zum Thema

Bisher haben wir von Autos mit Pedalantrieb gesprochen: wir wollen aber auch an ein anderes System der Fortbewegung erinnern, das damals, ein bißchen in Anlehnung an den Rudersport, ausprobiert wurde, allerdings mit mäßigem Erfolg. Eine Notiz darüber finden wir beispielsweise in einer Werbeanzeige der Firma Winkel aus Batavia, in der ein Kinderfahrzeug mit Namen "Vliegende Hollander" angeboten wurde, das mit der Kraft der Arme statt mit der der Beine fortbewegt wurde. Dieses Kinderfahrzeug hatte wahrhaftig wenig mit dem Automobil außer den vier Rädern gemeinsam. Selbst in England wurde diese Art von "kart", ohne Karosserie und mit Armantrieb, in den

Le "coda a pinna"

Anni del primo dopoguerra: siamo alla vigilia di eventi importanti anche per le "bébé auto". Parallelamente all'incalzante sviluppo dell'automobile, si assiste, in tutti i maggiori paesi, ad un fuoco di fila di iniziative, talune anche memorabili, che entreranno a far parte della storia del costume. Mentre sino a qualche tempo prima, questi giocattoli, salvo taluni casi, erano sommarie riproduzioni di automobili vere, ora si segue con sempre maggiore attenzione la realtà ed i cataloghi si arricchiscono continuamente di sorprese per far sognare ad occhi aperti i futuri automobilisti.

Dopo la stasi imposta dalla guerra le corse sono riprese ovunque con rinnovato slancio: gli autodromi di Brooklands, Indianapolis, Monza, Montlhéry, le innumerevoli gare su strada richiamano folle straboccchevoli e lo sport del volante, con i suoi leggendari campioni, manda alle stelle l'entusiasmo della gente.

La febbre si trasmette dai grandi ai piccoli ed i costruttori di "bébé auto" non si fanno certo cogliere impreparati dagli eventi. Una delle caratteristiche delle vetturette da corsa degli anni venti è la coda a punta, che si rifà allo stile dei bolidi del tempo.

La marca francese Eureka è una stella di prima grandezza nel firmamento delle "bébé auto" e tale rimarrà per tutto il ventennio fra le due guerre: nei suoi cataloghi le vetturette da corsa hanno sempre avuto un posto di spicco e la moda delle coda a punta si ritrova in diversi esemplari. Anche fra la produzione della italiana Giordani, della inglese Triang e della americana Steelcraft, tanto per citare qualche caso, viene ripreso questo disegno attinto dal mondo delle corse.

Sia fatta la luce

Un nuovo elemento concorre a dare un ulteriore tocco di realismo alle "bébé auto" degli anni venti: l'impiego dell'energia elettrica. Le primitive auto per bambini, nei pochi casi in cui disponevano di fanali, montavano copie simulate: tuttavia qualche esemplare molto raffinato arrivò a montare piccole lanterne ad olio.

Nel 1922 la "bébé auto" con fari elettrici funzionanti a batteria è ormai una realtà; non servono a molto perché il suo conducente alla sera non va ancora al "tabarin", ma con quelle lampadine accese si sente certo più importante — oggi si direbbe più realizzato — e la distanza che lo separa dal papà si riduce ancora.

Dai fari al motore. L'utilizzazione dell'energia elettrica nelle "bébé auto" era logico si estendesse anche alla trazione ed ecco così una nuova conquista negli annali dei ruggenti anni venti: le prime auto per bambini con motore elettrico.

Fortunatamente il loro costo era alto e ciò ne limitò la diffusione: in tal modo venne garantita la sopravvivenza a quel sano esercizio muscolare che i pedali comportano.

Piccole auto, grandi nomi

Negli anni Venti l'impegno di tutti i costruttori è rivolto a migliorare ulteriormente le "bébé auto" e ad imitare sempre più le auto vere. Negli Stati Uniti le numerose fabbriche, che hanno invaso il mercato con una marea di vetturette sempre più suggestive, spendono con molta facilità i nomi delle grandi Case automobilistiche, mentre i fabbricanti europei si mostrano in proposito assai più prudenti.

La American National Company, ad esempio, presenta nel 1925 una splendida Packard coupé per bambini completamente chiusa, la Boycraft uno spider con la scritta Cadillac, mentre un contemporaneo catalogo della Steelcraft è cosparso dei nomi di Buick, Nash, Studebaker, Lincoln, Pierce Arrow, Marmon, Chrysler e perfino Mack, dato che non di rado nei cataloghi comparivano dei "bébé camion".

known as "Moko". Among the other pedalcars-with lever or block chain transmission appeared a small vehicle operated by two handles placed rather unattractively on the bonnet.

"Pointed tails"

The first years after the war were a time of important events in general and also for our "cars for kids". Parallel with the rapid development of the motorcar, there was a burst of initiative in all major countries, producing in some cases memorable results which were to take on historic significance. Whereas, up to a short time before, these toys were on the whole simplified reproductions of real cars, now a lot more attention was paid to the originals and catalogues were constantly showing exciting new models to thrill young drivers.

After the standstill imposed by the war, the car business got back into full swing with renewed energy everywhere; the racing tracks at Brooklands, Indianapolis, Monza and Montlhéry and numerous competitions on the street focused people's attention once again onto this crazy sport of driving which, with its legendary heroes, drove people wild with enthusiasm.

This feverish enthusiasm about car racing passed on to pedal-cars too, and manufacturers certainly didn't let themselves be caught unprepared. One characteristic of model racing cars of the twenties was the pointed tail, which was also a characteristic of very fast racing cars of the time. The French trademark Eureka was one of the greatest names in the world of "cars for kids" and remained so throughout the twenty years between the two wars; in its catalogues these small racing cars always occupied a prominent position, and the fashion of the pointed tail appeared on several models. This design, taken from the world of racing, also appeared in some models produced by the Italian company Giordani, the English Triang and the American Steelcraft.

Let there be light

A new element helped give a final touch of realism to the "cars for kids" of the twenties: the use of electricity. In the few cases of early model cars which boasted lights, they were simply fake ones, except for a few very sophisticated models which were provided with small oil lamps.

In 1922 "cars for kids" with electric lights running on batteries became a reality. They did not serve much purpose since the drivers of these cars had not yet reached the stage of going off on night-time jaunts; nevertheless those little lights lit-up certainly gave the driver a feeling of importance. The whole experience of driving became more "real" as it were, and the distance separating the child driver from the grown-up was reduced still more.

From the lights to the motor. It was a logical step to extend the use of electricity to the traction too, and thus came about a new conquest of the roaring twenties: the first cars for children with electric motors. Fortunately their cost was high and so their popularity was limited, and in this way the survival of the healthy muscular exercise of pedalling was guaranteed.

Small cars, big names

The job of all manufacturers in the twenties was, ultimately, to improve their "cars for kids" in terms of their likeness to real cars. In the United States, the numerous factories, which had flooded the market with a sea of increasingly effective model cars, freely used the names of the big car manufacturers, while their European counterparts were far more prudent in this sense.

In 1925 for example the American National Company produced a splendid, completely enclosed Packard coupé for children, Boycraft

actionnée par deux manivelles placées sur le capot, et dont l'esthétique laisse à désirer.

Les "arrières pointus"

La guerre vient de s'achever et les autos juniors aussi sont à la veille d'événements importants. Avec le développement rapide de l'automobile, on assiste dans la plupart des pays, à un véritable feu roulant d'initiatives dont certaines joueront d'ailleurs un rôle mémorable dans l'évolution des moeurs. Tandis qu'auparavant ces jouets n'étaient, à quelques exceptions près, que des reproductions sommaires de véritables automobiles, ils sont maintenant de plus en plus fidèles à la réalité et les catalogues s'enrichissent constamment de nouvelles surprises à faire rêver les futurs automobilistes.
Après la pause imposée par la guerre, les courses automobiles reprennent de toutes parts avec un nouvel élan. Les circuits de Brooklands, Indianapolis, Monza, Montlhéry, et les nombreuses courses sur route attirent les foules qui accueillent le sport automobile et ses champions légendaires avec des transports d'enthousiasme. La fièvre se transmet aux petits et les fabricants d'autos juniors ne se font certes pas prendre au dépourvu. Les petites voitures de course des années vingt se caractérisent par l'arrière en pointe, imitant la ligne des bolides de l'époque.
La marque française Euréka est une étoile de première grandeur au firmament des autos juniors et le restera pendant les vingts années de l'entre-deux-guerres. Dans les catalogues, les petites autos de course ont toujours occupé une place d'honneur et la mode de l'arrière en pointe, empruntée au monde des courses, se retrouve dans divers modèles comme chez Giordani en Italie, Triang en Angleterre et Steelcraft aux Etats Unis, pour ne citer que quelques noms.

Que la lumière soit

Un nouvel élément contribue à donner une touche de réalisme aux autos juniors des années vingt: l'énergie électrique. Jusque là, les phares faisaient généralement défaut sur les petites voitures et, lorsqu'ils étaient montés, ce n'étaient que de vulgaires copies, sauf sur quelques modèles très raffinés qui furent équipés de petites lanternes à huile.
En 1922, les autos juniors avec phare électriques fonctionnant à pile, sont désormais une réalité. Il est vrai qu'ils ne servent pas à grand chose, le petit automobiliste ne sortant pas encore le soir pour faire la "Tournée des Grands Ducs" mais, avec ces lampes allumées il se sent certainement plus important — on dirait aujourd'hui plus réalisé — et la distance qui le sépare de papa se réduit d'autant.
Des phares, on passe au moteur. Il était logique que l'électricité soit également appliquée au système de traction. Et voilà une nouvelle conquête dans les annales de ces années folles: les premières petites voitures à moteur électrique sont apparues. Leur prix était heureusement trop élevé pour en permettre une grande diffusion: le sain exercice musculaire procuré par les pédales n'aurait certainement pas survécu!

Petites voitures et grands noms

Tous les fabricants des années vingt ont pris à coeur d'améliorer ultérieurement les autos juniors et d'imiter de plus en plus fidèlement les vraies automobiles. Aux Etats-Unis, les nombreuses firmes qui ont inondé le marché d'une marée de petites voitures de plus en plus évocatrices, ont emprunté en toute liberté les noms de grands constructeurs automobiles, tandis que les fabricants européens se montraient beaucoup plus prudents.
Par exemple, American National Company présente en 1925, un magnifique coupé Packard miniature et entièrement fermé, la firme Handel gebracht; er hieß dort "Empire Racer" und wir finden ihn auch in den Katalogen der Vereinigten Staaten: hier war er als "Hand car" oder auch "Irish Mail" bekannt. Wahrscheinlich erweckte er keine großen Sympathien, weil er das Auge wenig befriedigte. Ein anderes kurioses Antriebssystem ist das, das in einem Katalog der Zwanzigerjahre der deutschen Fabrik Kohnstamm zu sehen ist, bekannt auch als "Moko". Unter den anderen Tretmodellen mit Hebel- oder Kettenübertragung tritt in der Tat ein Autochen auf, das durch zwei ziemlich unschöne Handkurbeln auf der Kühlerhaube angetrieben wird.

"Spitzheck" Autos

Die ersten Jahre der Nackriegszeit: wir befinden uns am Vorabend bedeutender Ereignisse auch für das Kinderauto. Im Gleichschritt mit der stürmischen Entwicklung des Automobils wohnt man in allen größeren Ländern einer schnell aufeinanderfolgenden Reihe von Initiativen bei, die manchmal auch denkwürdig sind und in die Geschichte der Sitten und Gebräuche eintreten. Während bis einige Zeit zuvor diese Spielzeuge mit einigen Ausnahmen summarische Reproduktionen echter Automobile waren, folgt man der Wirklichkeit jetzt mit immer größerer Aufmerksamkeit, und die Kataloge bieten immer mehr Überraschungen, die die zuküftigern Autofahrer bei offenen Augen träumen lassen. Nach dem durch den Krieg bedingten Stillstand wurden die Autorennen überall mit neuem Schwung wieder aufgenommen: die Rennbahnen von Brooklands, Indianapolis, Monza, Montlhéry, die unzähligen Straßenrennen ziehen ungeheure Zuschauermengen an, und der Autorennsport mit seinen legendären Helden treibt die Begeisterung auf die Spitze. Das Rennfieber überträgt sich von den Großen auf die Kleinen, und die Hersteller der Kinderautos lassen sich von der Ereignissen sicher nicht unvorbereitet überraschen. Eines der Kennzeichen der kleinen Reunwagen der Zwanzigerjahre ist das Spitzheck, das sich an den Stil der Rennautos der damaligen Zeit anlehnt. Die französische Marke Eureka ist ein Stern erster Größenordnung am Firmament der Kinderautos, und sie bleibt es während der ganzen zwanzig Jahren zwischen den beiden Weltkriegen: in ihren Katalogen nehmen die Kinderrennautos immer einen herausragenden Platz ein und die Mode des Spitzhecks findet man in verschiedenen Exemplaren. Auch in der Produktion der italienischen Firma Giordani, der englischen Triang und der amerikanischen Steelcraft, um nur einige Fälle aufzuführen, wird dieses aus der Rennsportwelt übernommene Design aufgenommen.

Es werde Licht

Ein neues Attribut trägt dazu bei, dem Kinderauto der Zwanzigerjahre einen weiteren realistischen Aspekt zu verleihen: nämlich die Verwendung des elektrischen Stromes. In den seltenen Fällen, in denen die ersten Kinderautos, über Scheinwerfer verfügten, handelte es sich um Attrappen: einige sehr raffinierte Exemplare allerdings hatten schon kleine Öllaternen montiert. Im Jahre 1922 sind Kinderautos mit elektrischen, batteriebetriebenen Scheinwerfern numehr eine Realität. Sicher haben sie keinen großen Nutzen, da der Fahrer abends keine Nachbars besuchen fährt, aber mit den erleuchteten Scheinwerfern fühlt er sich gewiß wichtiger - heute würde man sagen erfüllt - und der Abstand, der ihn von seinem Vater trennt - wird weiter vermindert.
Von den Scheinwerfern zum Motor. Es war nur folgerichtig, daß die Verwendung des elektrischen Stroms bei den Kinderautos sich auch auf den Antrieb ausweitete, und so haben wir eine neue Errungenschaft in der Geschichte der tollen Zwanzigerjahre: die ersten Kinderautos mit Elektromotor. Glücklicherweise waren die Kosten sehr hoch, was die Verbreitung dieses Fahrzeugs einschränkte: und so wurde jener gesunden Muskelübung, die die Pedale mit sich bringen, das Überleben gewährleistet.

Che poi a tutti questi modelli corrispondessero altrettante automobili vere è ancora da dimostrare: però i nomi ci sono e servono a far presa sul pubblico dei giovanissimi.
Ford, Chevrolet, Dodge "fire chief" sono ancora definite qualche anno dopo altre vetturette per bambini, che in America è di moda chiamare "Juvenile Automobiles" o anche "Wheel Goods Toys", definizione più generica che comprendeva ogni tipo di veicolo per bambini azionato a pedali o a braccia.
Una "bébé auto" italiana in legno, che ricorda una "509" carrozzata Weymann, reca sul frontale il marchio Fiat e una Casa tedesca, la Moko, arriva a piazzare sul radiatore di una sua vetturetta la stella a tre punte, senza peraltro nominare la Mercedes-Benz. C'è chi invece fa leva sui dettagli: la Toledo americana, reclamizzando in una inserzione del 1924 un suo modello genericamente definito "De Luxe" mette in evidenza una ventina di particolari tecnici ed estetici destinati a richiamare l'attenzione della clientela.

L'auto come papà

André Citroën, uomo geniale e con idee d'avanguardia, fu uno dei primi capitani d'industria a vedere nell'automobile giocattolo un eccellente veicolo pubblicitario per una Casa automobilistica e nel bambino un suo potenziale cliente. Il bambino — egli sosteneva — doveva imparare a dire da piccolo tre parole "papà, mamma e Citroën"; giocando con la sua auto in miniatura non doveva dire "la mia auto", ma "la mia Citroën". Forte di questo suo convincimento l'industriale francese iniziò una grossa operazione promozionale intesa ad accattivarsi le simpatie dei piccoli, operazione che durò diversi anni e che portò alla creazione dei famosi "Jouets Citroën", oggi tra i pezzi più ricercati dai collezionisti. Per dare un'idea della serietà di questo sforzo, basti dire che in una decina d'anni un'officina specializzata legata alla Citroën costruì oltre mezzo milione di giocattoli meccanici di grande formato destinati ai figli dei clienti della Casa.
Nella quasi totalità si trattava di giocattoli in lamiera in scala 1:10 ma, in due riprese, nel 1925 e nel 1928, Citroën uscì con due "bébé auto" che fecero epoca. La prima fu una fedele riproduzione della "5HP" Treflé, che apparve quasi contemporaneamente al lancio del modello vero: la prima "Citroënnette" era una graziosa auto a pedali in robusta lamiera lunga m. 1,50 con châssis a longheroni; qualche tempo dopo venne presentata la versione "grand luxe" con fari elettrici, rifiniture in cuoio, pneumatici speciali e variatore di velocità. Un esemplare della piccola "5HP" venne data a tutti i Concessionari Citroën.
Tre anni dopo assistiamo ad un salto di qualità: la Citroën presenta la "C4", magnifica riproduzione in scala 1:3 per bambini. Questa volta il motore elettrico ha preso il posto dei pedali: la piccola cabriolet viaggia a quasi 15 Km h., dispone di marcia avanti e retromarcia, fari e claxon. L'automobile come papà non è più un sogno.

Si divertono piccoli e grandi

Il caso Citroën non è unico. L'occhio interessato dei grandi si è ormai posato sulle "bébé auto", che non costituiscono più caccia riservata dei bambini.
Tante volte sotto un innocente giocattolo ritroveremo un sottile strumento pubblicitario. La Bugatti "35" Grand Prix è una vettura da corsa favolosa che non finisce più di collezionare vittorie e ha portato alle stelle il nome del suo costruttore: logico che avesse un posto d'onore anche fra le "bébé auto". A provvederci è lo stesso Ettore Bugatti che nel 1927 costruisce un fedele modello della tipo "35" per suo figlio Roland: la vetturetta, provvista di motore elettrico e nota come "Baby Grand Prix Tipo 52", è la copia perfetta della celebre vettura da corsa: dai cerchioni al caratteristico radiatore, dalle cinghie sul cofano al posto di guida.

produced a spider with the name Cadillac on it, while a Steelcraft catalogue of the same year is strewn with names: Buick, Nash, Studebaker, Lincoln, Pierce Arrow, Marmon, Chrysler and even Mack, given that it was not rare for catalogues to include "lorries for kids". Whether there was a real car used as a model in each of these cases is a point yet to be proven; however the names were there and served to attract the young public.
Ford, Chevrolet, and Dodge "firechief" were more names given to other cars for children in the next few years. In America it became fashionable to call these cars "Juvenile Automobiles or "Wheel Goods Toys" which was a vaguer term and included any type of vehicle for children operated by pedals or by the arms.
An Italian pedal-car, made of wood, which recalls the body of a Weymann "509", bears the name Fiat on the front, and a German firm, Moko, even put on the radiator of one of its models a three-pointed star without however actually naming Mercedes-Benz. Other companies on the other hand played on details: Toledo, the American company, in an advertisement of 1924 for one of its models vaguely defined as "De Luxe", pointed out about twenty technical and aesthetic particulars destined to attract the public's attention.

A car like dad's

André Citroën, a very clever man with avant-garde ideas, was one of the first leaders of the industry to see in the toy car an excellent means of publicity for car manufacturers and to regard children as future clients. Children, he said, should learn to say right from the start three words: "daddy, mummy, and Citroën"; and while playing with their miniature cars, they should not say "my car" but "my Citroën". Convinced of this, the French industrialist started a huge promotional operation, aimed at winning the hearts of the young.
It was an operation that lasted several years and it brought into existence the famous "Jouets Citroën", which are today among the most sought-after collectors' pieces. To give an idea of the seriousness of this enterprise, it will suffice to say that, in ten years, a special department connected to Citroën made over half a million large mechanical toys destined for the sons of Citroën clients. Almost all of these were metal toys made on a scale of 1:10, but on two occasions, in 1925 and 1928, Citroën came out with two model cars which were true landmarks. The first was a faithful reproduction of a "5HP" Treflé, which appeared almost at the same time as the launching of the actual motorcar. This first "Citroënnette" was an attractive pedal-car in strong metal, 1,50 metres long with a side-frame chassis. Some time after the "grand luxe" model was produced, and this had electric lights, leather finishings, special tyres and speed variator. One of these "5HP" models was given to all Citroën concessionaries.
Three years afterwards there was a jump in quality; Citroën produced the "C4", a magnificent reproduction for children on a scale of 1:3. This time pedals were replaced by an electric motor; this small convertible travelled at almost 15 kmph, had forward and reverse gears, lights and a hooter. The car like dad's was no longer a dream.

Young and old enjoy themselves

Citroën was not alone. Other people now began to look at these "cars for kids" with more attention, as they could no longer be considered of interest only to children.
Very often we find in an innocent toy a subtle advertising instrument. The Bugatti "35" Grand Prix was a marvellous racing car which went on and on winning races and so made its maker famous; it was only natural that it would also have a place of honour among "cars for kids". In fact it was Ettore Bugatti himself who constructed in 1927 a faithful model of

Boycraft, un spider portant l'inscription Cadillac, tandis qu'un catalogue contemporain de chez Steelcraft est parsemé de noms comme Buick, Nash, Studebaker, Lincoln, Pierce Arrow, Marmon, Chrysler et même Mack, vu qu'il n'était pas rare d'y trouver également des camions juniors. Encore faut-il démontrer que tous ces modèles ont eu leur équivalent en grand: mais les noms sont là et servent à appâter le jeune public.

Ford, Chevrolet, Dodge et "Fire Chief" entrent quelques années plus tard dans le monde des autos juniors, appelées en Amérique "Juvenile Automobiles" ou encore "Wheel Goods Toys": définition plus générale englobant tous les véhicules pour enfants, qu'ils soient actionnés à pédales ou par la force des bras.

Une auto junior italienne en bois, qui rappelle une "509" carrossée par Weymann, porte la marque Fiat sur la calandre, tandis que la firme allemande Moko, applique une étoile à trois branches sur le radiateur de l'un de ses modèles, sans cependant mentionner le nom de Mercedes-Benz. D'autres, au contraire, préfèrent soigner les détails: dans un encart publicitaire de 1924, Toledo présente un modèle défini "de Luxe", en attirant l'attention de sa clientèle sur une vingtaine de détails techniques et esthétiques.

Une voiture comme papa

André Citroën, homme génial et toujours à la pointe du progrès, fut l'un des premiers constructeurs à comprendre que l'auto junior était un excellent véhicule publicitaire pour un contructeur automobile et que l'enfant devenait ainsi un client potentiel. Les trois premiers mots prononcés par un enfant — affirmait-il — devaient être "papa, maman et Citroën"; en parlant de son auto miniature, il ne devait plus dire "ma voiture", mais "ma Citroën". Convaincu de son idée, l'industriel français se lança dans une campagne promotionnelle destinée à gagner la sympathie des plus jeunes.

Cette opération dura plusieurs années et porta à la création des fameux "Jouets Citroën", qui sont aujourd'hui des pièces extrêmement recherchées par les collectionneurs. Pour mieux se rendre compte de l'importance de cet effort, il suffit de dire qu'en une dizaine d'années, un atelier spécialisé lié à Citroën fabrica plus de cinq cent mille jouets mécaniques de grande taille destinés aux enfants des clients de la Maison.

Il s'agissait, pour la plupart, de jouets en tôle reproduits à l'échelle 1:10. A deux reprise, en 1925 puis en 1928, Citroën créa des autos juniors qui firent époque. La première était une fidèle reproduction de la "5HP tréflé", qui sortit pratiquement au même moment que le modèle pour adultes: la première "citroënnette" était une ravissante et robuste voiture à pédales, mesurant 1,50 mètre de long et équipée d'un châssis à longerons; un peu plus tard, ce modèle sortit en version "grand luxe", avec phares électriques, finitions en cuir, pneus spéciaux et variateur de vitesse. Un exemplaire de la petite "5HP" fut alors offert à tous les concessionnaires Citroën.

Trois ans plus tard, un autre saut de qualité avec l'apparition d'une magnifique reproduction de la "C4", à l'échelle 1:3. Cette fois, le moteur électrique a pris la place des pédales: le petit cabriolet frôle les 15km/h, dispose d'une marche avant et d'une marche arrière, da phares et d'un klaxon. L'automobile comme celle de papa n'est plus un rêve.

Petits et grands s'amusent

L'expérience Citroën n'est pas unique. Le regard des adultes se pose désormais avec intérêt sur les autos juniors qui cessent d'être la chasse gardée des enfants.

Derrière un jouet apparemment innocent se cache souvent un subtil véhicule publicitaire. La Bugatti "35" Grand Prix est une voiture de course sans précédent qui collectionna victoire sur victoire et qui a porté

Kleine Autos, grosse Namen

In den Zwanzigerjahren bemühten sich die Hersteller, die Kinderautos weiter zu verbessern und immer mehr die echten Automobile nachzuahmen. In den Vereinigten Staaten verwenden die zahlreichen Kinderautofabriken, die den Markt mit einer Unzahl von immer verführerischeren Kinderautos überschwemmen, mit großer Leichtigkeit die Namen der bedeutenden Automobilfabriken, während die europäischen Hersteller hier ein vorsichtigeres Verhalten zeigen. Die American National Company beispielsweise führt 1925 ein vollständig geschlossenes Packard Coupé für Kinder vor, die Boycraft einen Spider mit der Aufschrift Cadillac, während ein gleichzeitiger Katalog der Steelcraft voll von Namen wie Buick, Nash, Studebaker, Lincoln, Pierce Arrow, Marmon, Chrysler und sogar Mack ist, da nicht selten in den Katalogen auch Kinderlastwagen aufgeführt waren. Daß allen diesen Modellen dann auch ebensoviele echte Autos entsprochen hätten, ist noch zu beweisen: die Namen jedoch existieren und dienen dazu, das Publikum der ganz Jungen zu beindrucken. Ford, Chevrolet, Dodge "fire chief" werden noch einige Jahre später andere Kinderautos genannt, die in Amerika gewöhnlich unter der Bezeichnung "Juvenile Automobiles" oder auch "Wheel Goods Toys" laufen, einer allgemeineren Definition, die jeden Typ von durch Pedale oder die Muskelkraft der Arme angetriebenen Fahrzeugen für Kinder mit einbegriff.

Ein italienisches Kinderauto aus Holz, das an einen "509" mit Karosserie Weymann erinnert, trägt auf dem Bug die Marke Fiat, und eine deutsche Firma, Moko, plazierte auf dem Kühler ihres Kinderautos sogar den dreizackigen Stern, ohne allerdings Mercedes-Benz zu nennen. Andere Firmen versuchen wieder durch Details zu beeindrucken: die amerikanische Firma Toledo wirbt in einer Anzeige von 1924 für eines ihrer allgemein "De Luxe" definierten Modelle, indem sie ungefähr zwanzig technische und ästhetische Details anführt, die dazu bestimmt sind, die Aufmerksamkeit der Kundschaft zu erregen.

Ein Auto wie Papa

André Citroën, ein genialer Mann mit avantgardistischen Ideen, war einer der ersten Industriellen, der im Spielzeugauto ein ausgezeichnetes Mittel der Werbung für eine Automobilfabrik und im Kind einen potentiellen Kunden sah. Das Kind - so behauptete er - sollte von klein auf drei Wörter lernen: "Papa, Mama und Citroën"; wenn es mit seinem Miniaturauto spielte, durfte es nicht sagen: "mein Auto" sondern "mein Citroën". Von dieser Tatsache überzeugt, begann der französische Industrielle eine große Werbekampagne, die darauf abzielte, die Sympathien der Kleinen für sich zu gewinnen, eine Kampagne, die verschiedene Jahre lang dauerte und die zur Schaffung der berühmten "Jouets Citroën" führte, die heute zu den gesuchtesten Stücken für Sammler zählen. Um eine Vorstellung davon zu geben, mit welcher Ernsthaftigkeit diese Aktion durchgeführt wurde, genügt es zu erwähnen, daß in einem Zeitraum von ungefähr zehn Jahren eine mit Citroën verbundene spezialisierte Werkstatt über eine halbe Million von großformatigen mechanischen Spielsachen baute, die für die Kinder der Kunden des Automobilwerkes bestimmt waren. Fast zum größten Teil handelte es sich dabei um Blechspielzeug im Maßstab 1:10, zweimal jedoch, 1925 und 1928, gab Citroën zwei epochemachende Kinderautos heraus. Das erste war eine naturgetreue Nachbildung des "5 HP" Treflé und erschien fast gleichzeitig mit seinem Vorbild auf dem Markt: die erste "Citroënnette" war ein anmutiges Tretauto aus kräftigem Blech, 1,50 m lang, mit einem Längsträgerfahrgestell; einige Zeit darauf wurde die "grand luxe" Ausführung mit elektrischen Scheinwerfern, Lederverarbeitung, Spezialgummireifen und Gangschaltung vorgestellt. Ein Exemplar des kleinen "5 HP" wurde an alle Vertragshändler von Citroën geliefert. Drei Jahre darauf wohnen wir einer sprunghaften Verbesserung

Realizzato il prototipo, Bugatti passa alla piccola serie: di questo giocattolo di sogno vennero fabbricati in tutto una novantina di esemplari, che andarono ai figli dei suoi clienti più facoltosi.
Negli anni a cavallo del 1930, in Francia specialmente, vennero organizzate moltissime gare e concorsi di eleganza che ebbero come protagoniste le graziose "tipo 52" del mago di Molsheim. La fama della Bugatti "35" era però troppo grande per non stimolare l'interesse di altri costruttori: versioni a pedali della celebre vettura, di vario prezzo, furono prodotte dalla francese Eureka, alla quale va il merito di aver portato il nome Bugatti anche nei giardini e nei parchi gioco dei bambini.
Altro caso di parentela fra una "bébé auto" e una Casa automobilistica è quello che si registrò in Italia nel 1928, quando Guido Cattaneo, dell'ufficio tecnico della Isotta Fraschini, mise in cantiere due vetturette denominate ABC e destinate ai figli dell'amministratore delegato della Società. Provviste di un motore Peugeot a quattro cilindri di 700 cc., complete di freni a tamburo, vero radiatore e altre raffinatezze, erano qualcosa di più di una "bébé auto" e, nelle intenzioni dei costruttori, dovevano superare il capolavoro di Ettore Bugatti. Dei due esemplari, uno, acquistato dal corridore Trossi e da lui modificato nella carrozzeria, si trova oggi conservato al Museo dell'Automobile di Torino.

I piccoli re

Il dono alla moda per gli eredi di sangue reale, i figli di personaggi importanti, i rampolli di illustri casati fu, specie negli anni fra le due guerre, appunto la "bébé auto": non un modello qualunque, ma quasi sempre un pezzo unico costruito appositamente o in serie limitata. Gli episodi non si contano.
La Rivista Autocar, nell'aprile del 1932, ci mostra una mini Rolls Royce speciale donata alla Principessa Elisabetta, poi Regina d'Inghilterra, dalla Lines Bros. In Motor del maggio 1938 c'è la foto di un Maragià indiano che prova una vetturetta Rytecraft Special destinata a suo figlio. Due Hispano Suiza 1927, con tanto di motore elettrico e velocità di circa 40 Kmh., furono costruite appositamente per i bambini della famiglia Esders, i re delle confezioni. E c'è anche una Panhard 6 cilindri in miniatura che la Casa francese offrì nel 1934 al figlio del Sultano del Marocco. Due Citroën "traction avant" gemelle furono donate nel 1937 alle Principesse Margaret ed Elisabetta d'Inghilterra e una stupenda Cadillac 1916 in miniatura andò al figlio del Re di Thailandia.

L'età d'oro

Mentre i pargoli dei re ricevono doni da favola senza sborsare un quattrino, la gente comune è disposta a qualsiasi sacrificio pur di vedere i propri figli al volante di una "bébé auto" anche noleggiata e non rinuncia all'ambizione di immortalarne le prime imprese automobilistiche sulla lastra di uno di quei fotografi ambulanti che una volta stazionavano nei viali dei giardini pubblici.
Sempre più tentatrice, la "bébé auto" pare non abbia risentito della grande crisi ed anzi i modelli seguono da vicino il progresso dell'automobile e la sua evoluzione stilistica. Negli anni trenta, che possiamo senz'altro considerare l'età d'oro delle "bébé auto", in Francia sono in vendita bellissime copie a pedali di Peugeot e Renault del momento con carrozzeria monoblocco, ruote in gomma, sedili regolabili, luci e claxon elettrici per bimbi da 2 a 7 anni; c'è perfino una eccellente riproduzione della "Petite Rosalie" da record che nel 1933 conseguì una serie di primati mondiali sulla pista di Montlhéry. Le linee aerodinamiche dell'epoca non tardano ad apparire nei cataloghi delle "bébé auto": la Triang, oltre a modelli di stile tradizionale, come le belle Rolls Royce 1930, Vauxhall 1932 e Daimler 1938, propone, quasi allo scoppio della guerra, una vetturetta tipo "Airflow", mentre nel 1938 la Troy di Philadelphia offre ai giovani automobilisti una serie di vetturette col

the "35" for his son Roland; this model car, provided with an electric motor and listed as the "Baby Grand Prix Type 52" was a perfect copy of the famous racing car: from the hub caps to the characteristic radiator, from the straps on the bonnet to the driving seat. Having created his prototype Bugatti went on to produce a small series; about ninety models of this dream toy were produced which were to go to the sons of his most wealthy clients.
Around 1930, particularly in France, a lot of competitions and "elegance" contests were organised in which the attractive "tipo 52" models belonging to the "wizard" of Molsheim took part. The fame of the Bugatti "35" was too great not to stimulate the interest of other car manufacturers; pedal versions of the famous car, at various prices, were produced by the French firm Eureka to whom the merit goes of having taken the name Bugatti into parks and children's playgrounds.
Another case of kinship between a car for children and a motorcar manufacturer was in Italy in 1928 when Guido Cattaneo, from the technical office of Isotta Fraschini, designed two model cars named ABC which were destined for the sons of the deputy manager of that firm. Each provided with a 700cc four cylinder engine, complete with drum brakes, a real radiator and other refinements, they were something more than "cars for kids", and were intended by the makers to outdo the masterpiece created by Ettore Bugatti. One of the two models was bought by the racing driver Trossi; he made slight changes to the engine and to the body, and the car can be seen today in the Museo dell'Automobile in Turin.

Little kings

The fashionable gift for royal heirs, for the sons of important people and the offspring of anyone famous was, especially in the years between the two wars, a model car: not any old model but almost always a unique model made especially or at least produced only in a limited series. Of such stories, there are many examples.
Autocar magazine shows us in the April 1932 edition a special mini Rolls Royce which was presented to Princess Elizabeth, the future queen of England, by Lines Bros. In Motor of May 1938 there is a photograph of an Indian maharajah who is trying out a Rytecraft Special model car which was destined for his son. Two Hispano Suiza 1927 model cars with electric motors and a speed of about 40kmph were made especially for the children of the Esders family, the well known clothes manufacturers. And there was also a miniature six cylinder Panhard which the French Marque gave to the son of the Sultan of Marocco in 1934. Two identical "traction avant" Citroëns were given to the Princesses Margaret and Elizabeth of England and a stupendous miniature Cadillac 1916 went to the son of the King of Thailand.

The golden age

While the children of kings were receiving these fairy-tale gifts without paying out a penny, many ordinary people were still prepared to make some sacrifice in order to see their own children at the wheel, even if this meant hiring a car; and it was possible to have these first driving endeavours immortalised by one of those wandering photographers who used to set themselves up along the paths of public gardens.
"Cars for kids" were increasingly more tempting, apparently not having been affected by the great depression, and they closely followed the progress of the motorcar and its stylistic evolution. In the thirties, which we can certainly consider as the golden age of "cars for kids", there were on sale in France some beautiful pedal models of Peugeot and Renault cars of that time; they had monobloc bodies, rubber wheels, adjustable seats, electric lights and hooters, and were suitable for children between two and seven years old. There is even an excellent reproduction of the

au firmament le nom de son constructeur: il fallait bien lui faire occuper cette place d'honneur parmi les autos juniors. Et c'est Ettore Bugatti lui-même qui s'en chargea. En 1927, il fabriqua une fidèle reproduction de sa "35" pour son fils Roland; la petite voiture à moteur électrique connue sous le nom de "Baby Grand Prix Type 52", est la copie parfaite de la célèbre auto de course. Rien ne manque: des jantes au radiateur caractéristique, du poste de pilotage aux courroies sur le capot. Après avoir réalisé ce prototype, Ettore Bugatti passe à une petite série d'environ quatre-vingt-dix fantastiques exemplaires qui deviendront les jouets de rêve des enfants des clients les plus fortunés.

Autour de 1930, nombre de courses et de concours d'élégance furent organisés, spécialement en France, avec les gracieuses "type 52" du magicien de Molsheim comme protagonistes. La Bugatti "35" était cependant trop célèbre pour ne pas stimuler l'intérêt d'autres fabricants: de nombreuses versions à pédales, pour toutes les bourses, furent ainsi produites par la Maison française "Euréka" à qui revient le mérite d'avoir porté le nom de Bugatti dans les parcs et les jardins d'enfants. Un autre exemple de la parenté entre une auto junior et une marque automobile nous vient d'Italie lorsqu'en 1928, Guido Cattaneo, du bureau technique d'Isotta Fraschini, construisit deux petites voitures appelées ABC et destinées aux deux enfants de l'administrateur délégué de la Société. Equipées d'un moteur Peugeot à quatre cylindres de 700 cm^3, de freins à tambour, d'un véritable radiateur et de nombreux autres raffinements, ces voitures étaient plus que des autos juniors, car elles devaient dépasser le chef-d'œuvre d'Ettore Bugatti, dans l'intention des constructeurs. Un des deux exemplaires, acheté par le coureur Trossi qui apporta des modifications au moteur et à la carrosserie, est actuellement conservé au Musée de l'Automobile de Turin.

Les petits rois

Pendant l'entre-deux-guerre, l'auto junior était le cadeau à la mode pour les héritiers de sang royal, les enfants de personnages importants et les fils de familles illustres. Mais pas un modèle quelconque, il s'agissait presque toujours d'un exemplaire unique ou produit en toute petite série. Les exemples ne manquent pas.

La revue Autocar du mois d'avril 1932 nous illustre une mini Rolls Royce, spécialement créée par la Maison Lines Bros pour l'offrir à la Princesse Elisabeth, future Reine d'Angleterre. Dans la revue Motor de mai 1938, figure la photo d'un Maharadjah essayant une petite Rytecraft Special destinée à son fils.

Deux modèles Hispano Suiza, équipés d'un moteur électrique permettant d'atteindre la vitesse de 40km/h, furent spécialement conçus en 1927 pour les enfants de la famille Esders, le roi de la confection. Et c'est toujours une auto junior, une Panhard 6 cylindres miniature, que la firme française offrit, en 1934, au fils du Sultan du Maroc. Les Princesses Margaret et Elisabeth d'Angleterre reçurent également en 1937 deux modèles Citroën traction avant absolument identiques, tandis qu'une splendide Cadillac 1916 en miniature fut offerte au fils du Roi de Thaïlande.

L'âge d'or

Alors que les enfants de sang royal reçoivent de fabuleux cadeaux sans bourse délier, le commun des mortels est prêt à tous les sacrifices pour voir ses enfants au volant d'une auto junior, même louée, et ne renonce pas à l'ambition d'immortaliser leurs premières aventures sur la plaque de l'un des nombreux photographes ambulants qui sillonnaient jadis les boulevards et les jardins publics.

De plus en plus attrayante, l'auto junior ne semble pas avoir souffert de la grande crise; bien au contraire, les modèles suivent de près les progrès de l'automobile et l'évolution de son style. Pendant les années trente, qui

der Qualität bei: Citroën stellt seinen "C 4" vor, eine großartige Nachbildung im Maßstab 1:3 für Kinder. Dieses Mal hat ein Elektromotor die Stelle der Pedale eingenommen: das kleine Cabriolet erzielt eine Reisegeschwindigkeit von fast 15 km/st, verfügt über Vorwärts- und Rückwärtsgang, Scheinwerfer und Hupe. Ein Auto wie das Papas ist kein Traum mehr.

Klein und Gross amüsiert sich

Der Fall Citroën steht nicht allein da. Das interessierte Auge der Erwachsenen hat sich numehr den Kinderautos zugewandt, die nicht mehr eine bloße Jagdreserve der Kinder darstellen. Oft finden wir hinter einem unschuldigen Spielzeug ein raffiniertes Mittel der Werbung. Der Bugatti Typ "35" Grand Prix ist ein fabelhaftes Rennauto, das nicht aufhört, Siege zu sammeln und das den Namen seines Konstrukteurs in den Himmel erhoben hat: es ist nur folgerichtig, daß er auch unter den Kinderautos einen Ehrenplatz einnimmt. Dafür sorgt Ettore Bugatti selbst, der 1927 für seinen Sohn Roland ein naturgetreues Modell des Typs "35" konstruiert: das kleine mit einem Elektromotor versehene und als "Baby Grand Prix Tipo 52" bekannte Auto ist das perfekte Abbild des berühmten Rennwagens: von den Felgen zum typischen Kühler, von den Riemen auf der Motorhaube zum Fahrersitz. Nach Fertigstellung des Prototyps geht Bugatti zur kleinen Serie über: von diesem Traumspielzeug werden insgesamt ungefähr neunzig Exemplare angefertigt, die für die Söhne seiner zahlungskräftigsten Kunden bestimmt waren. In den Jahren um 1930 herum werden besonders in Frankreich viele Rennen und Eleganzwettbewerbe organisiert, die den anmutigen "Typ 52" des Zauberers von Molsheim als Hauptperson vorstellen. Der Ruf des Bugatti "35" war allerdings zu groß, um nicht das Interesse der anderen Konstrukteure zu erwecken: eine Tretausführung des berühmten Wagens in verschiedenen Preislagen wurde von der französischen Firma Eureka hergestellt, der das Verdienst zukommt, den Namen Bugatti auch in Parks und auf Kinderspielplätzen eingeführt zu haben. Ein weiterer Fall von Verwandtschaft zwischen einem Kinderauto und einer Automobilfabrik ist der, der 1928 in Italien vermerkt wurde, als Guido Cattaneo aus dem Technischen Büro der Isotta Fraschini zwei ABC genannte kleine Autos bauen ließ, die für die Söhne des Geschäftsführers der Gesellschaft bestimmt waren. Ausgestattet mit einem Peugeot-Motor mit vier Zylindern und 700 ccm Hubraum, Trommelbremsen, einem echten Kühler und weiteren Raffinessen, waren sie etwas mehr als bloße Kinderautos und sollten nach der Absicht der Erbauer das Meisterwerk Ettore Bugattis übertrumpfen. Eines der beiden Exemplare, das von dem Rennfahrer Trossi erworben und von ihm in Motor und Karosserie verändert worden war, wird heute im Automobilmuseum von Turin aufbewahrt.

Die kleinen Könige

Das Modegeschenk für die Erben königlichen Geblüts, die Kinder bedeutender Persönlichkeiten und die Sprößlinge berühmter Häuser war, besonders in den Jahren zwischen den beiden Welktriegen, eben das Kinderauto: natürlich kein x-beliebiges Modell, sondern fast immer ein Einzelstück, das extra oder in begrenzter Serie hergestellt wurde. Die Fälle sind unzählbar. Die Zeitschrift Autocar vom April 1932 zeigt uns einen Mini Rolls Royce in Spezialanfertigung, der der Prinzessin Elisabeth, der späteren Königin von England, von der Lines Bros geschenkt worden war. In der Zeitschrift Motor vom Mai 1938 ist die Photographie eines indischen Maharadschas zu sehen, der ein für seinen Sohn bestimmtes Miniaturauto Rytercraft Special ausprobiert. Zwei Hispano Suiza von 1927, beide mit Elektromotor ausgestattet und mit einer Höchstgeschwindigkeit von ungefähr 40 Stundenkilometer, wurden extra für die Kinder der Familie Esders, des Königs der Konfektion,

caratteristico "musone a spartivento", che contraddistinse tutta un'epoca a cavallo della guerra.

Babbo Natale torna dal fronte

La guerra imporrà una battuta d'arresto anche alle "bébé auto" ma, appena spentasi l'eco delle cannonate, il mondo dei giocattoli è pronto a rimettersi in moto con rinnovato slancio per festeggiare i primi Natali di pace.
In Inghilterra nel 1949 si registra subito un episodio significativo: si apre la Austin Junior Car Factory cioè un apposito stabilimento adibito alla fabbricazione di auto per bambini che dovrà dar lavoro a 200 ex minatori invalidi. I modelli in cantiere sono la "twin cam" da corsa e la "J40", due vetturette a pedali di pregevole fattura che rimarranno in produzione per una ventina d'anni.
In un primo tempo le fabbriche sopravvissute si limitano a riprodurre modelli del passato ma, con gli anni cinquanta, si assiste ovunque ad un fiorire di nuove iniziative. Sorgono altre piccole industrie, la tecnica si evolve, i modelli vengono aggiornati. Il legno è ormai un ricordo del passato; per qualche tempo le carrozzerie sono quasi tutte ancora in metallo, ma l'era della plastica è ormai iniziata.
L'impiego del polistirolo, del Moplen, del PVC e poi della fibra di vetro, consentendo una riduzione dei costi e quindi prezzi più bassi, contribuirà da una parte alla diffusione sempre più massiccia delle "bébé auto", ma dall'altra darà luogo, specie nella grande serie, ad un appiattimento della qualità. Le nuove vetturette hanno poco in comune con le loro antenate degli anni venti e trenta, che si distinguevano per quel tocco artigianale e quel pizzico di ingenuità, che tanto piaccino ai collezionisti di oggi.
Il "boom" automobilistico fa prosperare anche l'industria delle auto per bambini che sforna novità senza posa: alcuni sono modelli di fantasia, altri ricalcano linee di auto vere e fra queste incontrano molto favore i bolidi da corsa tipo Ferrari, Lotus, Cooper ecc. Gli esemplari più economici funzionano sempre a pedali; col passare del tempo però si vanno diffondendo anche le vetturette provviste di motorini elettrici, ora prodotte a prezzi popolarissimi.
Ma questa è già storia di oggi.

Le auto di sogno

Fin qui i prodotti di serie. Un capitolo a parte meritano invece quelle piccole meraviglie su quattro ruote che vengono alla ribalta di tanto in tanto facendo sognare ad occhi aperti i giovani, sia pur così disincantati, dei nostri giorni.
Negli ultimi decenni, in vari paesi del mondo, si sono avute numerose interessanti iniziative in questo settore, che hanno suscitato viva curiosità anche fra gli adulti. Parliamo di quelle vetturette costruite in serie limitata che sono la fedele riproduzione di automobili vere; azionate da motori elettrici o a scoppio, talvolta sfruttando le strutture meccaniche dei "karts", dispongono quasi sempre di un complesso di accessori e di particolari costruttivi che ne fanno non più un giocattolo, ma spesso una vettura in piena regola.
Molte volte queste vetturette sono servite per organizzare divertenti competizioni sportive, concorsi, manifestazioni all'aperto dove il bambino è chiamato a fare la parte del protagonista. Ricordare tutti questi episodi non è certo possibile: ci limiteremo a citarne alcuni lasciando parlare le immagini.
In Italia, dove l'automobilismo ha tradizioni illustri, le vetturette fuori classe sono state molte: nel 1949 il costruttore Piero Patria esce con una singolare auto elettrica a tre ruote deniminata "Lucciola" e tre anni dopo costruisce in pochi esemplari una magnifica riproduzione per bambini della Cisitalia Grand Prix 1947 con motore a scoppio mentre nel 1956

"Petite Rosalie" on record, which in 1932 made a series of world records on the racing track at Montlhéry. The aerodynamic lines of the period soon appeared in catalogues of children's cars: Triang, besides traditionally styled models like the beautiful Rolls Royces of 1930, the Vauxhalls of 1932 and the Daimlers of 1938, put forward, almost on the eve of the war, an "Airflow" model car, while in 1938 Troy of Philadelphia was offering young drivers a series of model cars with the characteristic wind-divider "nose" which marked a whole period around the war.

Father Christmas returns from the front

The war imposed a certain standstill even upon the production of "cars for kids", but hardly had the echo of the canons died away than the world of toys was ready to put itself back into action with renewed strength to celebrate the first Christmasses of peacetime.
In England in 1949 there was a significant event: the Austin Junior Car Factory opened, a special factory set aside for the manufacture of cars for children which would give work to 200 disabled ex-miners. The models on the production line were the racing "twin cam" and the "J40", two beautifully made pedal-cars which remained in production for about twenty years.
Initially the surviving manufacturers limited themselves to producing models of the past but, with the fifties, there was a flowering of initiative everywhere. More small industries were set up, the technical side developed and models were up-dated. Wood was now a thing of the past; for some time almost all car bodies had still been made of metal, but the age of plastic had already begun.
The employment of polystyrene, of Moplen, of PVC and then of fibreglass allowed a reduction in costs which meant lower prices, and contributed on the one hand to the ever greater popularity of "cars for kids" but on the other, particularly in mass produced lines, was responsable for a worsening of quality. The new model cars had little in common with their ancestors of the twenties and thirties, which were notable for their craftsmanship and that certain touch of ingeniousness which are so much admired by collectors today. The motorcar "boom" also helped the children's cars industry prosper and an increasing number of novelties were turned out. Some of these were imaginary models, others imitated real cars, among which fast racing cars like Ferrari, Lotus, Cooper met with great favour. The cheapest models were still operated by pedals; as time went on however, those cars with small electric motors also gained in popularity, and are now produced at very reasonable prices.
But that is already present day history.

Dreamcars

From then on, cars for children were mass produced. But still every so often a small miracle on four wheels has come to light; and despite the general disillusionment of the young nowadays, these few outstanding models have still produced excitement and wonder.
In the last ten years there has been a lot of initiative taken in this field in various parts of the world, and the interest of adults has also been aroused. We shall speak now of those model cars which have been produced in limited editions and which are faithful reproductions of real cars. Operated by electric motors or combustion engines, or now and then profiting from the mechanical structure of the "go-kart", they have nearly always been provided with a set of accessories and details of construction which have made them something more than toys; often they have been vehicles in the true sense.
Very often these cars have been used in the organisation of interesting outdoor sports competitions or exhibitions, in which children have been

représentent sans aucun doute l'âge d'or des autos juniors, de splendides copies à pédales destinée aux enfants de 2 à 7 ans, reproduisent les derniers modèles Renault et Peugeot de l'époque. Ces exemplaires, en vente sur le marché français, ont une carrosserie monobloc, des roues à bandagede caoutchouc, des sièges réglables, des phares et un klaxon électriques. On trouve même une excellente copie de la "Petite Rosalie" qui a battu une série de records du monde sur le circuit de Montlhéry en 1933. Les lignes aérodynamiques de l'époque ne tardent pas à faire leur apparition dans les catalogues d'autos juniors. En plus de ses modèles de style traditionnel, comme les ravissantes Rolls Royce 1930, Vauxhall 1932 et Daimler 1938, la firme Triang crée une petite voiture type "Airflox" à la veille de la deuxième guerre mondiale. A Philadelphie, en 1938, Troy offre aux jeunes automobilistes une série de petites voitures au "long museau" fendant le vent, caractéristique de l'avant et de l'après-guerre.

Le Père Noël revient du front

Pendant la guerre, les autos juniors ont, elles aussi, marqué un temps d'arrêt, mais dès que le bruit des canons se tait, le monde des jouets renaît avec une vigueur renouvelée pour fêter les premiers Noëls de paix. Un épisode significatif nous vient de Grande Bretagne avec la fondation, en 1949, de l'Austin Junior Car Factory. Il s'agit d'un atelier se consacrant exclusivement à la production d'autos juniors et qui permettra d'employer 200 mineurs invalides. Les modèles produits sont la "twin cam" de course et la "J40", deux petites voitures à pédales d'excellente facture qui resteront en production pendant une vingtaine d'années.

Dans un premier temps, les ateliers rescapés se limitèrent à reproduire des modèles du passé mais, avec les années cinquante, de nouvelles initiatives fleurissent de partout. D'autres petites industries voient le jour, la technique évolue et les modèles se modernisent. Le bois n'est alors qu'un souvenir; mais si pendant quelques années, les carrosseries sont presque toutes métalliques, l'ère du plastique a désormais commencé.

Le polystyrène, le Moplen, le PVC, puis la fibre de verre, permettent de réduire considérablement les coûts de production. Alors que les autos juniors, bien moins chères, prolifèrent, on assiste à un nivellement de la qualité, spécialement pour les voitures produites en grande série. Les modèles modernes ont bien peu de choses en commun avec leurs ancêtres des années vingt et trente qui, elles, se distinguaient par la touche artisanale et le grain de naïveté que les collectionneurs d'aujourd'hui apprécient tant.

Le "boom" de l'automobile se répercute sur l'industrie des autos juniors qui ne cesse d'offrir des nouveautés. La ligne peut être imaginaire ou reproduire celle de véritables automobiles, comme les bolides de course type Ferrari, Lotus, Cooper, etc., pour ne citer que ceux qui remportent le plus grand succès. Les modèles les plus économiques sont encore à pédales, mais les voitures équipées d'un moteur électrique se répandent de plus en plus et sont vendues à des prix extrêmement populaires. Nous entrons désormais dans l'histoire récente.

Des autos de rêve

Voilà pour les modèles produits en série, mais une parenthèse s'impose pour les petites merveilles à quatre roues qui, de temps à autre, font leur apparition en faisant rêver les enfants d'aujourd'hui, qui semblent pourtant déjà tous blasés.
Ces dix dernières années ont vu de nombreuses initiatives dans ce domaine, en suscitant un vif intérêt, même de la part des adultes. Nous voulons parler de ces voitures miniatures, fabriquées en petites séries, qui sont la fidèle reproduction de véritables automobiles; actionnées par

angefertigt. Dann ist da noch ein Panhard Sechszylinder in Miniatur, den die französische Firma 1934 dem Sohn des Sultans von Marokko anbot. Zwei identische Citroën "Vorderradantrieb", wurden 1937 den Prinzessinen Margaret und Elisabeth von England geschenkt und einen phantastischen Cadillac Baujahr 1916 in Miniatur erhielt der Sohn des siamesischen Königs als Geschenk.

Das goldene Zeitalter

Während die Königskinder märchenhafte Geschenke erhalten, ohne einen Pfennig auszugeben, ist der Mann von der Straße zu jedem Opfer bereit, nur um seine Kinder am Steuer eines - auch gemieteten - Kinderautos zu sehen, und er verzichtet nicht auf sein ehrgeiziges Vorhaben, sie auf die Platte eines jener ambulanten Fotografen bannen zu lassen, die damals in den Alleen der öffentlichen Parkanlagen ihren Stand aufgeschlagen hatten. Von immer größerer Verführungskraft, scheint es, daß das Kinderauto nichts von der Weltwirtschaftskrise verspürt hat, im Gegenteil, die Modelle folgen Schritt auf Schritt der technischen und stilistischen Entwicklung des Automobils. In den Dreißigerjahren, die wir ohne Zweifel als das "Goldene Zeitalter des Kinderautos" ansehen können, stehen in Frankreich wunderschöne Nachahmungen der damaligen Renault- und Peugeotmodelle als Tretautos mit Karosserie aus einem Block, Gummirädern, verstellbaren Sitzen, elektrischen Scheinwerfern und Hupen für Kinder von 2 bis 7 Jahren zum Verkauf; es gab sogar eine ausgezeichnete Reproduktion des Renwagens "Petite Rosalie", der 1933 auf der Rennbahn von Montlhery eine Reihe von Weltrekorden aufstellte. Die damaligen Stromlinienformen erscheinen bald in den Katalogen der Kinderautos: die Firma Triang schlägt, außer den Modellen im traditionellen Stil wie die schönen Rolls Royce von 1930, den Vauxhall von 1932 und Daimler von 1938, fast bei Ausbruch des Krieges ein kleines Auto vom Typ "Airflow" vor, während 1938 die Firma Troy aus Philadelphia den jungen Autofahrern eine Serie von Autochen mit der typischen windschnittigen "Schnauze" anbietet, die die ganze Epoche um den 2. Weltkrieg herum charakterisierte.

Der Weihnachtsmann kommt von der Front zurück

Der Krieg brachte auch für die Kinderautos einen Stillstand mit sich, aber kaum war das Echo der Kanonen verstummt, als die Welt des Spielzeugs schon wieder bereit ist, sich mit erneuertem Schwung in Gang zu setzen, um das erste Weihnachtsfest der Friedenszeit zu begehen. In England spielt sich 1949 sofort eine bedeutsame Episode ab: die Eröffnung der Austin Junior Car Factory, d.h. eine extra zur Herstellung von Kinderautos eingerichtete Fabrik, die 200 Kriegsinvaliden, ehemaligen Bergleuten, Arbeit geben sollte. Die in Produktion befindlichen Modelle sind der "twin cam", ein Rennautochen und der "J 40", zwei Tretautos von vortrefflicher Machart, die ungefähr zwanzig Jahre lang hergestellt werden.

Zunächst beschränken sich die Fabriken, die den Krieg überlebt hatten, auf die Reproduktion von Modellen der Vergangenheit, in den Fünfzigerjahren aber bemerkt man überall ein Aufblühen neuer Initiativen. Es entstehen weitere kleine Industrieunternehmen, die Technik entwkelt sich, die Modelle werden auf den letzten Stand gebracht. Das Material Holz gehört nunmehr der Vergangenheit an; eine gewisse Zeit lang sind fast alle Karosserien noch aus Metall, allerdings hat das Zeitalter der Kunststoffe schon begonnen. Die Verwendung von Polystyrol, Moplen, PVC und dann Glasfiber bringen eine Herabsetzung der Kosten und somit eine Verringerung der Preise mit sich und trägt somit einerseits zu einer immer größeren Ausbreitung der Kinderautos bei, führt aber andererseits, besonders in großer Serienherstellung, zu einer Nivellierung der Qualität. Die neuen Kinderautos haben wenig mit

appare la "Bimbo Racer" elettrica della Sila; è poi la volta di alcune repliche di auto veterane, della Mini Alfa Disneyland, della Mini Lotus di Canni Ferrari con motore a scoppio, tutte degli anni sessanta, per arrivare alla "Ferrarina 77" con motore a scoppio, che era la copia della "312 T2" di Lauda, e alla Jeep Bimbo Racer.

Nel 1955 un industriale californiano costruisce a Lawndale un piccolo autodromo dove corrono minuscole "midget" con motore a scoppio pilotate da bambini. Parecchie interessanti iniziative nel campo delle auto per bambini si devono al francese Francis Mortarini, un valoroso restauratore di auto d'epoca che, dopo aver messo assieme una straordinaria collezione di "bébé auto" blasonate, decise di passare alla produzione di pezzi d'alta classe. La Ferrari "330 P2" che vinse a Le Mans nel 1964, venne da lui mirabilmente riprodotta in scala l'anno dopo: aveva un motore a scoppio, carrozzeria in vetroresina, telaio tubolare, freni a disco. Fu poi la volta di un altro piccolo capolavoro: la Ford "GT 40". Un gruppo di queste vetturette diede vita nel 1966 ad una originale gara per ragazzi, la "24 Minuti", che precedeva la più famosa "24 Ore" di Le Mans.

Un'altra vetturetta importante, con motore a benzina, uscì in Inghilterra negli anni sessanta: riproduceva fedelmente la famosa Jaguar "D"; si chiamava "Cheetah Cub Car" ed era costruita dalla Glass Fibre. Pure inglese e della stessa epoca una Cooper in miniatura con motore a scoppio di 20 cc., opera di Jack Knight.

Ancora dalla Francia un esemplare di rilievo: la Star "55" realizzata nel 1977 dalla Arola e riproducente la Bugatti "55" Super Sport 1932. Degli ultimi anni sono le suggestive vetture inglesi della Lely, che ripropone tra l'altro la famosa Citroën "5 HP" del 1924 anche in versione furgoncino, e della Hamilton Brooks che ha messo a punto una spettacolare Williams Saudia Formula 1 con motore elettrico.

E concludiamo questa nostra rapida carrellata con le favolose vetturette costruite in Svizzera da Franco Sbarro. La prima, del 1975, è la replica della BMW "328", la seconda riproduce la Mercedes-Benz "540 K" e la terza la Ferrari "Testa Rossa".

Con caratteristiche differenti fra loro, sono tutte equipaggiate con motore a scoppio, hanno carrozzeria in vetroresina, impianto freni, luci. La "Testa Rossa" è una vettura in piena regola, per ragazzi di circa 15 anni, lunga m. 3,30, viaggia a 90 kmh. Presentate ogni anno al Salone dell'Automobile di Ginevra, hanno riscosso particolari simpatie tra la figliolanza dei magnati del petrolio; un dato soltanto basta a confermarlo: in una reggia del Medio Oriente ci sono ben venti Mercedes "540K" in miniatura circolanti.

I papà ereditano la passione

Negli ultimi anni, in diversi Paesi, si è assistito ad un fenomeno curioso: le "bébé auto" usate o scampate alla distruzione dei bambini, sono passate è di proprietà dal figlio al padre. In altre parole è nata, come per gli altri giocattoli, la moda del collezionismo.

Oggi esistono al mondo moltissimi collezionisti e Musei che posseggono queste vetturette: è naturale che, più sono vecchie, più sono ricercate e se per caso hanno anche un blasone, come certe "bébé auto" appartenute a figli di personaggi importanti, il loro valore diventa inestimabile. Il francese Francis Mortarini, in quasi vent'anni di pazienti e anche fortunate ricerche e valendosi della sua abilità di restauratore, riuscì a mettere assieme una eccezionale raccolta di vetturette di gran razza, che negli anni sessanta presentò in diverse occasioni. Erano per lo più pezzi unici appartenuti in passato a famiglie illustri, da lui ritrovati, talvolta costati cambi molto onerosi con vetture d'epoca e infine perfettamente restaurati.

Questo di Mortarini, come pochi altri, deve tuttavia essere considerato un caso limite: logicamente la maggior parte degli appassionati si accontenta di pezzi di minore importanza, ma non per questo meno

asked to play the leading roles. It is certainly not possible to list all of these events so we will limit ourselves to mentioning one or two and let the photographs speak for themselves.

In Italy, where motoring has famous traditions, there have been many outstanding model cars produced. In 1949 Piero Patria, a car manufacturer, came out with an unusual three wheel electric car called "Lucciola", three years later he built only a few models of a magnificent reproduction for children of the Cisitalia Grand Prix 1947 with combustion engine; in 1956 appeared the electric "Bimbo Racer" made by Sila.

Then came the time of some replicas of veteran cars, of the Mini Alfa Disneyland, the Mini Lotus, the Canni. Ferrari with a combustion engine, all of which were produced in the sixties, to come finally to the "Ferrarina 77" with a combustion engine which was a copy of Lauda's "312 T2", and to the Jeep Bimbo Racer.

In 1955 a Californian industrialist built a small racing track at Lawndale where miniature "midgets" equipped with combustion engines could run, driven by children. Quite a lot of interesting enterprises in this field of children's cars were taken by the Frenchman Francis Mortarini, a gallant restorer of old cars, who after getting together an extraordinary collection of "titled" children's cars, decided to move on to actually producing top class models.

In 1965, he made an admirable scale model of the Ferrari "330 P2" which won at Le Mans in 1964: it had a combustion engine, a fibreglass body, a tubular chassis and disc brakes. After that it was time for another small masterpiece: the Ford "GT 40". In 1966 a group of these model cars were used to set up an original competition for children: it was called the "24 Minutes" and preceded the more famous "24 Hours" of Le Mans.

Another important model car, with an engine that ran on petrol, came out in England in the sixties; made of fibreglass, it was called the "Cheetah Cub Car" and was a close reproduction of the famous Jaguar "D". Also English, of the same period and built by Jack Knight, was a miniature Cooper with a 20cc. combustion engine.

From France again came another important model: the Star "55" made in 1977 by Arola, a reproduction of the Bugatti "55" Super Sport 1932. The last few years have seen the very effective model cars produced by the English Lely: these have been based, among others, on the famous Citroën "5HP" of 1924, which includes a model van version. Also in recent years there was the spectacular Williams Saudia Formula 1 for children, a car with an electric motor made and perfected by Hamilton Brooks. And we shall finish this rapid close-up view with the fabulous model cars made in Switzerland by Franco Sbarro. The first, made in 1975, is a copy of the BMW "328", the second reproduces the Mercedes Benz "540 K", and the third the Ferrari "Testa Rossa".

Each has its own individual characteristics, but all of them are equipped with combustion engines, fibreglass bodies and a system of brakes and lights. The "Testa Rossa" is a "real" car: designed for children of about 15 years old, it is 3.30 metres long, and travels at a speed of 90kmph. They are put on show every year at the Salon de l'Automobile in Geneva, and have met with particular interest among the offspring of oil magnates. One figure is enough to confirm this: in one royal palace in the Middle East there are a good twenty miniature Mercedes "540 K" in circulation.

Grown ups take over

In the last few years in various countries a curious phenomenon has occured: "cars for kids" having been used, but having escaped total destruction at the hands of children, have been passed on from son to father. In other words, the craze for collecting model cars, along with other toys, has begun.

Today there are a lot of museums and collections all over the world which

un moteur électrique ou à explosion et utilisant parfois les structures mécaniques des "karts", leurs caractéristiques et leurs nombreux accessoires en font non plus des jouets, mais presque toujours des automobiles à part entière.

Ces voitures ont souvent été utilisées pour d'amusantes compétitions sportives, des concours ou des manifestations en plein air où l'enfant est appelé à jouer le rôle principal. Il n'est certes pas possible de rappeler ici tous ces épisodes; nous nous limiterons à n'en citer que quelques-uns en laissant parler les images.

En Italie, pays où l'automobile a une tradition illustre, on trouve de nombreuses voitures hors-classe: en 1949 le constructeur Piero Patria présente une auto électrique singulière à trois roues appelée "Lucciola" et trois ans plus tard, il construit une magnifique reproduction pour enfants de la Cisitalia Grand Prix 1947 avec moteur à explosion en quelques exemplaires seulement; en 1956 on assiste à la sortie de la "Bimbo Racer" électrique construite par Sila. C'est ensuite le tour des répliques de plusieurs anciens modèles miniatures, comme la Mini Alfa Disneyland, la Mini Lotus et la Canni Ferrari, avec moteur à explosion, datant toutes des années soixante, pour arriver à la "Ferrarina 77" à moteur à explosion qui est la copie de la "312 T2" de Niki Lauda, puis à la Jeep Bimbo Racer.

En 1955, un industriel californien fait construire à Lawndale un circuit miniature sur lequel peuvent courir des enfants au volant de minuscules "midget" équipées d'un moteur à explosion. Plusieurs initiatives intéressantes dans le domaine des autos pour enfants, sont dues au français Francis Mortarini, un habile restaurateur de voitures d'époque qui, après avoir réuni une extraordinaire collection d'autos juniors portant blason, décida de passer à la production d'exemplaires de grande classe. Une magnifique reproduction à l'échelle de la Ferrari "330 P2", qui a remporté la victoire aux 24 heures du Mans en 1964, est ainsi réalisée l'année suivante: elle avait un moteur à explosion, une carrosserie en fibre de verre, un châssis tubulaire et des freins à disque. Puis ce fut le tour d'un autre petit chef-d'œuvre: la Ford "GT 40". En 1966, plusieurs de ces modèles seront les protagonistes d'un singulier événement aux mains de jeunes adolescents: la course des "24 Minutes" qui précéda celle, plus célèbre, des "24 heures" du Mans.

Dans les années soixante, un autre important modèle, avec moteur à essence, sort en Angleterre; il s'agit d'une fidèle reproduction de la fameuse Jaguar "D" de la firme Glass Fibre et qui a été baptisée "Cheetah Cub Car".

Toujours en Angleterre, et à la même époque, Jack Knight crée une Cooper miniature, équipée d'un moteur à explosion. En 1977, un autre exemplaire digne d'intérêt est fabriqué en France par Arola et reproduit la Bugatti "55" Super Sport 1932 sous le nom de Star "55". Pour ces dernières années, mentionnons les petites voitures anglaises très évocatrices de Lely qui repropose, entre autres, la fameuse Citroën "5HP" de 1924, dans sa version normale et camionnette, et de Hamilton Brooks qui a mis point une spectaculaire Williams Saudia Formule 1, équipée d'un moteur électrique. Nous terminons notre rapide tour d'horizon avec les fabuleuses voitures miniatures construites en Suisse par Franco Sbarro. La première, de 1975, est la réplique de la B.M.W. "328", la seconde reproduit la Mercedes-Benz "540" et la troisième, la Ferrari "Testa Rossa".

Bien que leurs caractéristiques diffèrent, elles sont toutes équipées d'un moteur à explosion, d'une carosserie en fibre de verre, de freins et de phares. La "Testa Rossa" est une véritable voiture destinée aux adolescents d'une quinzaine d'années; elle mesure 3,30 mètres et roule à 90 km/h. Présentées chaque année au Salon de l'Automobile de Genève, ces voitures ont obtenu un immense succès auprès des fils des magnats du pétrole. Un seul exemple suffit pout le confirmer: un palais du Moyen

ihren Ahnen der Zwanziger- und Dreißigerjahre zu tun, die sich durch jenen handwerklichen Einschlag und jenen Schuß von Naivität auszeichneten, die den heutigen Sammlern so sehr gefallen. Der "Boom" des Automobils begünstigt auch die Blüte der Kinderautoindustrie, die pausenlos neue Modelle herausbringt: einige sind Phantasieprodukte, andere ahmen die Linienführung echter Automobile nach, und unter diesen gewinnen die Gunst des Publikums die Rennwagen vom Typ Ferrari, Lotus, Cooper usw. Die billigsten Modelle funktionieren immer noch mit Pedalen; im Laufe der Zeit verbreiten sich immer mehr auch die mit kleinen Elektromotoren ausgestatteten Modelle, die zu sehr erschwinglichen Preisen hergestellt werden. Das ist allerdings schon Gegenwartsgeschichte.

Die Traumautos

Bis hierher die Serienprodukte. Ein Extrakapitel verdienen hingegen jene kleinen Wunderwerke auf vier Rädern, die von Zeit zu Zeit ins Rampenlicht gerückt werden und die jungen Leute unserer Tage, seien sie auch noch so illusionslos, bei offenen Augen träumen lassen. In den letzten Jahrzehnten wurden in verschiedenen Ländern der Erde zahlreiche interessante Initiativen auf diesem Gebiet unternommen, die auch unter den Erwachsenen eine lebhafte Neugierde erweckt haben. Wir sprechen hier von jenen in beschränkter Serie erbauten Modellen, die naturgetreue Nachbildungen echter Automobile darstellen; von elektrischen oder Verbrennungsmotoren angetrieben, verwenden sie manchmal die mechanischen Strukturen der "karts"; fast immer verfügen sie über einen Komplex von Zubehörteilen und Konstruktionsdetails, die aus ihnen kein Spielzeug, sondern ein regelrechtes Auto machen. Vielmals dienten diese kleinen Autos dazu, amüsante Rennen, sportliche Wettbewerbe, Veranstaltungen im Freien zu organisieren, wo das Kind als Hauptperson teilnimmt. Es ist sicher nicht möglich, alle diese Episoden aufzuführen: wir werden uns darauf beschränken, einige zu nennen und sonst die Bilder sprechen zu lassen.

In Italien, wo der Automobilsport eine beeindruckende Tradition aufweist, waren die außergewöhnlichen Modelle zahlreich: 1949 bringt der Konstrukteur Pierre Patria eine eigentümliches dreirädriges, "Lucciola" genanntes Elektroauto heraus und drei Jahre darauf in wenigen Exemplaren eine großartige Kinderausführung des Cisitalia Grand Prix 1947 mit Verbrennungsmotor, während 1956 der elektrische "Bimbo Racer" der Firma Sila auf den Markt kommt; dann sind wiederum einige Nachbildungen von Veteranen an der Reihe, vom Mini Alfa Disneyland, vom Mini Lotus und vom Canni Ferrari mit Verbrennungsmotor, alle aus den Sechzigerjahren, um schließlich zum "Ferrarina 77" mit Verbrennungsmotor, der eine Nachbildung des "312 T2" Laudas war, und zum Jeep Bimbo Racer zu gelangen.

1955 baut ein kalifornischer Industrieller in Lawndale eine kleine Rennbahn, auf der die winzigen "midget" - Autos mit Verbrennungsmotor, von Kindern gesteuert, Rennen fahren. Verschiedene interessante Initiativen auf dem Feld der Kinderautos gehen auf den Franzosen Francis Mortarini, einen tüchtigen Restaurator von Oldtimern, zurück, der, nachdem er eine außergewöhnliche Sammlung von Kinderautos aristokratischer Herkunft zusammengestellt hatte, sich entschloß, zur Herstellung von Modellen höchster Klasse überzugehen. Der Ferrari "330 P2", der in Le Mans 1964 gewonnen hatte, wurde von ihm im Jahr darauf maßstabsgetreu nachgebaut: er besaß einen Verbrennungsmotor, eine Glasfaserkarosserie, einen Rohrrahmen und Scheibenbremsen. Dann war ein weiteres kleines Meisterwerk an der Reihe: der Ford "GT 40". Eine Gruppe dieser kleinen Autos unternahm 1966 ein originelles Rennen für Jungen, die sogenannten "24 Minuten", das vor dem berühmteren "24-Stunden-Rennen" von Le Mans abgehalten wurde. Ein weiteres bedeutendes Mini-Auto mit Benzinmotor, kam in England in den Sechzigerjahren heraus: es gab getreu den berühmten Jaguar "D"

suggestivi: una delle fonti più ricche sono le aste, come quelle famose di Sotheby's Belgravia, dove non di rado vengono messe all'incanto vecchie "bébé auto" cariche di anni e talvolta con qualche acciacco. Il restauro di queste vetturette d'epoca è un altro aspetto avvincente di questo hobby che appassiona i grandi: talora da rottami arrugginiti destinati alla demolizione e sulla scorta di una precisa documentazione, abbiamo visto risorgere delle "bébé auto" che per tanti anni potranno ancora raccontare la loro storia.

Grazie appunto a questa piccola schiera di appassionati, alla loro paziente opera di ricerca, al loro amore per le vecchie cose, oggi possiamo dunque rivedere tanti giocattoli del passato, che altrimenti sarebbero scomparsi dalla faccia della terra. Ed è anche merito loro se oggi abbiamo potuto scrivere questo libro.

possess these model cars; it is only natural that the older the cars the more sought after they become, and if by any chance they also have a title, like certain cars which belonged to the sons of important people, they become priceless.

In nearly twenty years of patient but also lucky research, the Frenchman Francis Mortarini, making use of his skill in restoring old cars, succeeded in getting together an exceptional collection of big-name cars which he put on show on several occasions in the sixties. They were for the most part unique models which had in the past belonged to famous families; his work involved firstly finding the cars and then very often making a lot of alterations and carrying out repairs to make of them in the end perfectly restored models.

Mortarini's case however is fairly unusual; naturally the majority of enthusiasts content themselves with pieces of minor importance, though none the less charming for this. One of the richest sources of these cars are auctions, such as at the famous Sothebys of Belgravia where it is quite often possible to find in the sale old "cars for kids" suffering from the ravages of time and not in perfect working order.

The restoration of these old cars is another interesting aspect of this hobby which provokes enthusiasm among grown-ups. Sometimes from rusty wrecks destined for the scrap heap it has been possible, with the help of precise documentation, to perfectly reconstruct some of the old "cars for kids", thus giving them a new lease of life in which they will be able to tell their own story.

It is due to precisely this small group of enthusiasts, to their patient research and to their love of old things that we can today look again at so many toys of the past which would otherwise have disappeared from the face of the earth by now. And it is also thanks to them that we have been able to write this book now.

Orient, abrite une collection impressionante de vingt Mercedes-Benz "540K" miniatures, toutes en état de marche.

La passion leguee a papa

Ces dernières années, un phénomène curieux s'est produit dans divers pays: les autos juniors usagées ou rescapées de la destruction des enfants, sont passées des mains de l'enfant à celles du père. En d'autres termes, comme pour les autres jouets, la manie de la collection a contagié les autos juniors aussi.

De nos jours, de nombreux collectionneurs et Musées sont en possession de ces petites voitures; évidemment, plus elles sont anciennes, plus elles sont recherchées et si, par chance, elles portent un blason, comme certaines autos juniors ayant appartenu aux enfants de personnages importants, leur valeur devient inestimable.

Le français Francis Mortarini, après presque vingt années de patience, avec la chance de son côté dans ses recherches et un véritable don de restaurateur, a réussi à réunir une exceptionelle collection de petites voitures de grande classe, qu'il présenta à diverses occasions au cours des années soixante. C'était, pour la plupart, des pièces uniques ayant appartenu à d'illustres familles. Il les avait retrouvées, échangées parfois avec des voitures d'époque et enfin, parfaitement restaurées. L'exemple de Mortarini, doit cependant être considéré comme un cas limite. En général, la plupart des collectionneurs se contentent d'exemplaires moins importants, mais qui n'en sont pas moins évocateurs. L'une des sources les plus précieuses pour se procurer ces anciens modèles, est la vente aux enchères comme celle de Sotheby Belgravia, où il n'est pas rare de dénicher de vieilles autos juniors chargées d'ans qu'elles n'ont pas toujours bien supporté. La restauration de ces petites autos d'époque est un autre aspect captivant de ce hobby qui passionne les grands: on a vu des mains habiles, guidées par une documentation précise, faire renaître des épaves rouillées destinées à la démolition, mais qui pourront encore raconter leur histoire pendant de nombreuses années.

C'est grâce à ce clan de passionnés, à leur patience, à leurs recherches et à leur amour pour les vieilles choses, que nous pouvons aujourd'hui revoir tant de jouets du passé qui, sinon, auraient déjà disparu.

Et si nous avons pu écrire ce livre, une part de mérite leur en revient.

wieder; er nannte sich "Cheetah Cub Car" und wurde von der Firma Glass Fibre gebaut. Ebenfalls englisch und aus derselben Zeit stammend, gab es dann einen Miniatur-Cooper mit Verbrennungsmotor von 20 ccm Hubraum, ein Werk von Jack Knight.

Aus Frankreich wiederum stammt ein weiteres herausragendes Modell: der Star "55", 1977 von der Firma Arola verwirklicht, der den Bugatti "55" Super Sport von 1932 nachahmte. In jüngster Zeit kamen die beeindruckenden englischen Mini-Autos der Firmen Lely, die unter anderen den berühmten Citroën "5 HP" aus dem Jahre 1924 auch in Lieferwagenform vorstellte, und Hamilton Brooks heraus, die einen phantastischen Williams Saudia Formel 1 für Kinder mit Elektromotor herstellte. Wir wollen diese unsere kurze Übersicht mit den in der Schweiz von Franco Sbarro gebauten fabelhaften Kinderautos abschließen: das erste Modell von 1975 ist die Nachahmung des BMW "328", das zweite ein Mercedes-Benz "540 K" und das dritte der Ferrari "testa Rossa". Mit untereinander verschiedenen Merkmalen, haben sie Ausstattung mit Verbrennungsmotor, Glasfiberkarosserie, Brems- und Lichtanlage gemeinsam. Der "Testa Rossa" ist ein echtes Auto für Jungen von etwa 15 Jahren, 3,30 m lang, erreicht es eine Spitze von 90 km/st. Jedes Jahr werden sie beim Genfer Automobilsalon vorgestellt und erfreuen sich besonderer Beliebtheit bei den Kindern der Erdölmagnaten. Ein einziger Hinweis mag genügen, um dies zu beweisen: in einem Palast im Mittleren Orient fahren gut 20 Miniatur-Mercedes "540 K" herum.

Die Papas erben die Leidenschaft

In den letzten Jahren konnte man in verschiedenen Ländern einem seltsamen Phänomen beiwohnen: die gebrauchten Kinderautos oder die, die der Zerstörung durch sie entkommen sind, gingen von dem Besitz der Kinder auf den des Vaters über. Anders gesagt, wie für anderes Spielzeug, hat die Sammelmode auch auf sie übergegriffen. Heute gibt es auf der Welt viele Sammler und Museen, die diese Mini-Autos besitzen: dabei ist es klar, daß sie desto mehr gesucht werden, je älter sie sind, und wenn sie überdies noch ein Wappen aufweisen sollten, wie einige Kinderautos, die Kindern bedeutender Persönlichkeiten gehörten, dann wird ihr Wert unschätzbar. Dem Franzosen Francis Mortarini ist es in zwanzig Jahren geduldiger und auch glückbegünstigter Suche und auch unter Einsatz seiner Geschicklichkeit als Restaurator gelungen, eine außergewöhnliche Sammlung von Kinderautos bester "Rasse" zusammenzustellen, die er in den Sechzigerjahren zu verschiedenen Anlässen dem Publikum vorstellte. Es handelte sich zum größten Teil um Einzelstücke, die früher berühmten Familien gehört hatten, von ihm gefunden worden waren und ihm manchmal sehr kostspielige Tauschgeschäfte mit von ihm perfekt restaurierten Oldtimern eingebracht hatten. Der Fall Mortarini muß allerdings wie wenige andere als ein Grenzfall angesehen werden: natürlich begnügt sich der größte Teil der leidenschaftlichen Sammler mit Stücken geringerer Bedeutung, die aber deswegen nicht unbedingt weniger eindrucksvoll sind: eine der reichsten Quellen für die Sammler sind die Auktionen, wie jene berühmten von Sotheby Belgravia, wo nicht selten alte Kinderautos, bejart und oft auch mit einigen Gebrechen, versteigert werden. Die Restauration dieser Kinder-Oldtimer ist ein weiterer fesselnder Aspekt dieses Hobbys, das die Großen begeistert: manchmal haben wir aus verrostetem, zum Wegwerfen bestimmtem Schrott auf Grund einer genauen Dokumentierung Kinderautos wiedererstehen sehen, die noch so lange Jahre ihre Geschichte erzählen können. Dank eben dieser kleinen Schar von Kinderautobegeisterten und ihrer geduldigen Sucharbeit, ihrer Liebe für die alten Dinge, können wir heute also so viele Spielsachen der Vergangenheit wiedersehen, die sonst von der Erdoberfläche verschwunden wären. Und es ist auch ihr Verdienst, wenn wir heute dieses Buch haben schreiben können.

Una elegante vetturetta a pedali del 1906: era prodotta dalla marca di biciclette "Excelsior" della Casa olandese Wijtenburg di Vlissingen. Le piccole automobiliste sono la proprietaria Cornelia Verheul di Vlissingen e la sua amica Louise Ouwerkerk di Londra.

An elegant pedal-car of 1906: it was produced under the name of "Excelsior", a trademark already used for bicycles made by the Dutch firm Wijtenburg of Vlissingen. The young motorists are the owner Cornelia Verheul from Vlissingen and her friend Louise Ouwerkerk from London.

Une élégante voiture à pédales de 1906, produite par la fabrique de vélo "Excelsior" de la firme hollandaise Wijtenburg de Vlissingen. Les petites automobilistes sont la propriétaire, Cornelia Verheul de Vlissingen, et son amie Louise Ouwerkerk de Londres.

Ein elegantes Tretauto aus dem Jahr 1906: hergestellt von der Fahrradmarke "Excelsior" der holländischen Firma Wijtenburg in Vlissingen. Die beiden kleinen Autofahrerinnen sind die Besitzerin Cornelia Verheul aus Vlissingen und ihre Freudin Louise Ouwerkerk aus London.

USA 1907: una rudimentale auto a pedali americana a due posti che porta sul radiatore il nome Cadillac. Le ruote sono quelle dei tricicli dell'epoca.

U.S.A., 1907: a simple American two-seater pedal-car which bears on the radiator the name Cadillac. The wheels are like tricycle wheels of the period.

USA 1907: une rudimentaire voiture à pédales américaine a deux places portant la marque Cadillac sur le radiateur. Les roues sont celles des tricycles de l'époque.

USA 1907: ein rudimentales zweisitziges amerikanisches Tretauto, das auf dem Kühler den Namen Cadillac trägt. Die Räder sind die der damaligen Dreiräder.

White Flyer: un'altra vetturetta a pedali prodotta in America nel 1910 circa che prende il nome da una famosa marca automobilistica del tempo, di cui copia il cofano squadrato.

White Flyer: another pedal-car, made in America in about 1910. It uses the name of a famous motorcar of that time, and also copies the square-shaped bonnet.

White Flyer: une autre voiture à pédales produite aux Etats Unis en 1910 environ. Elle prend son nom d'une célèbre marque de voitures de l'époque dont elle imite le coffre carré.

White Flyer: ein weiteres ungefähr um 1910 in Amerika hergestelltes Tretautochen, das seinen Namen von einer berühmten damaligen Automobilmarke übernommen hat, von der es die viereckige Motorhaube kopiert.

Dal catalogo "The Fair" di Chicago del 1903: assieme a carretti, cavallucci a dondolo e altri giocattoli, ecco comparire le prime automobili a pedali i cui nomi di Tandem Cycle Wagon e Automobile Velocipede confermano la stretta parentela con i velocipedi.

From the 1903 catalogue "The Fair" of Chicago: here, along with carts, rocking horses and other toys, the first pedal-cars made their appearance. Their names, Tandem Cycle Wagon and Automobile Velocipede are evidence of the close connection with the velocipede.

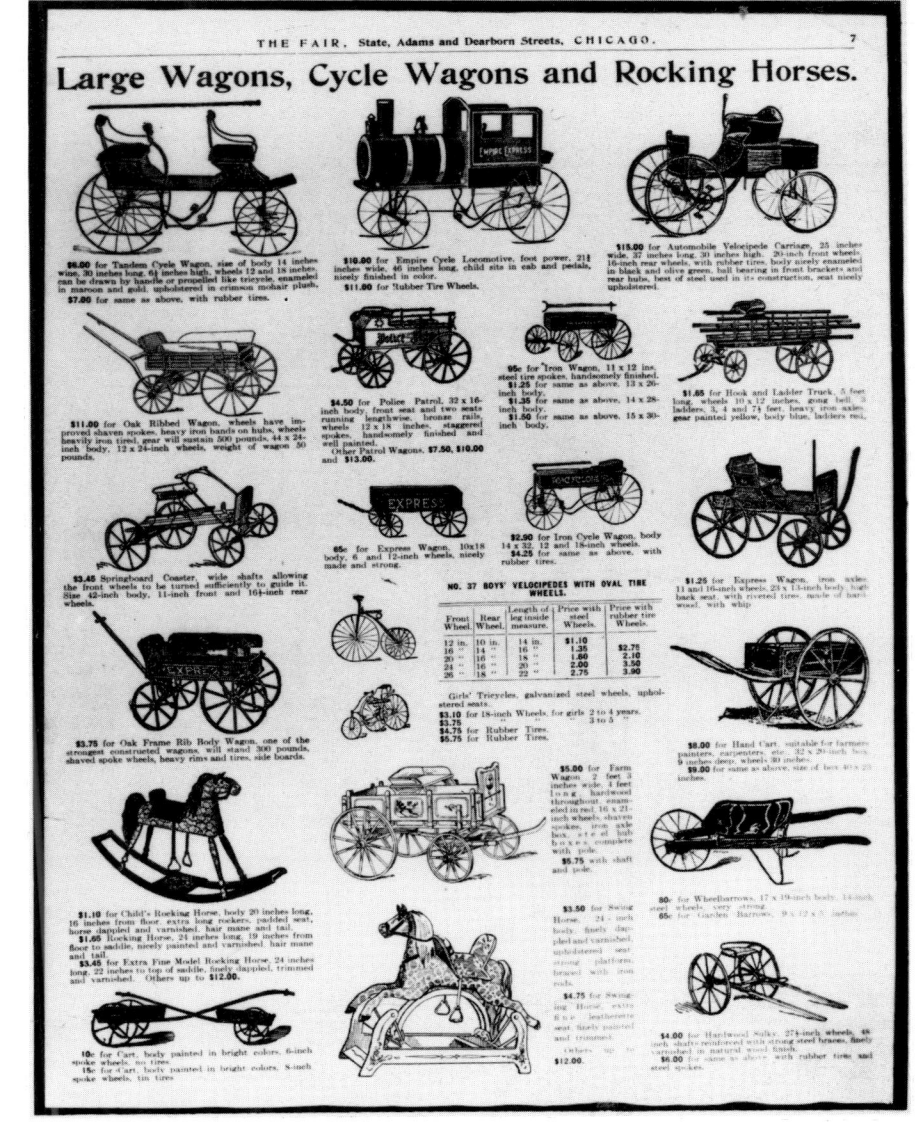

Una cartolina postale americana dei primi del Novecento in cui è simulato un incidente ad una vettura a pedali: la piccola automobilista è seriamente preoccupata per la perdita di una ruota.

An American postcard from the beginning of this century which shows a pedal-car "accident"; the young motorist is seriously worried because she has lost a wheel.

Une carte postale américaine du début du siècle simulant un accident de voiture à pédales; la petite automobiliste est sérieusement préoccupée par la perte d'une roue.

Eine amerikanische Postkarte aus den ersten Jahren unseres Jahrhunderts, auf der ein vorgetäuschter Unfall zwischen Tretautos dargestellt ist: die kleine Autofahrerin macht sich ernstlich Sorgen wegen des Verlusts eines Rades.

Tiré du catalogue "The Fair" de Chicago (1903): à côté des petites charrettes, des chevaux à bascule et autres jouets, apparaissent les premières autos à pédales; les noms de Tandem Cycle Wagon et d'Automobile Velocipede confirment leur étroite parenté avec les vélos.

Aus dem Katalog "The Fair", Chicago 1903: zusammen mit Schubkarren, Schaukelpferdchen und anderen Spielsachen werden die ersten Tretautos angeboten, deren Namen Tandem Cycle Wagon und Automobile Velocipede die enge Verwandtschaft mit den Fahrrädern bestätigen.

25

Più una carrozza senza cavalli che una vera automobile questa due posti per bambini degli albori del Novecento: classici elementi di origine ciclistica sono le ruote a raggi e la trasmissione a catena. La vetturetta è lunga m. 1,20.

This two-seater for children, from the very beginning of this century, is more a horseless carriage than a real car. The classic elements revealing its origins in the tricycle are the spoked wheels and the block chain drive. The model car is 1.20 metres long.

Plus proche d'un carrosse sans chevaux que d'une automobile proprement dite, cette deux places pour enfants remonte au début du siècle. Les roues à rayons et la transmission par chaîne sont autant d'éléments classiques d'origine cycliste. L'auto a une longueur de 1,20 m.

Eher einer Kutsche ohne Pferde als einem echten Automobil ähnelt dieser Kinderzweisitzer vom Beginn unseres Jahrhunderts: die Herkunft vom Fahrrad verraten die klassischen Bestandteile der Speichenräder und des Kettenantriebs. Das Autochen mißt 1,20 m.

Un accostamento irripetibile: nello stesso posto, nella stessa villa, alla stessa ora, nella stessa vetturetta a pedali a 70 anni di distanza, il conte Giovanni Lurani nel 1910 quand'era bambino e sempre lui in una foto del 1980. Questa auto a due posti venne costruita dalla carrozzeria Riva, le cui origini risalgono ai primi dell'Ottocento.

An unrepeatable match: in the same place, same house, and the same pedal-car but 70 years apart, these pictures show count Giovanni Lurani in 1910 as a child and then again in 1980. This two-seater car was made by the coachmakers Riva, whose origins go back to the early 1800s.

Une combinaison unique: au même endroit, dans la même villa, à la même heure et dans la même auto à pédales à 70 ans de distance: le comte Giovanni Lurani enfant en 1910 et toujours lui sur une photo de 1980. cette auto à deux places était fabriquée par la carrosserie Riva dont l'origine remonte au début du dix-neuvième siècle.

Eine nicht wiederholbare Kombination: am selben Ort, in derselben Villa, zur selben Tageszeit, in demselben Tretautochen, nur daß 70 Jahre dazwischenliegen: Graf Giovanni Lurani 1910, als er ein Kind war, und auf einem Foto von 1980. Dieser Zweisitzer wurde von der Karosseriewerkstatt Riva, die zum Beginn des 19. Jahrhunderts gegründet wurde gebaut.

Una foto scattata negli Stati Uniti verso il 1919 che ci mostra un'altra vetturetta per bambini del periodo pionieristico. Il piccolo autista sembra piuttosto soddisfatto della sua "bébé auto".

A photo taken in the United States around 1919 which shows us another car for children from the early days. The young driver looks very satisfied with his little car.

Une photo prise aux Etats Unis vers 1919 qui nous montre une autre voiture de l'époque héroïque. Le petit chauffeur semble plutôt satisfait de son auto.

Ein in den Vereinigten Staaten um 1919 geschossenes Foto zeigt uns ein weiteres Kinderauto aus der Pionierzeit. Der kleine Autofahrer scheint mit seinem "Baby-Auto" wirklich zufrieden zu sein.

Una delle più vecchie auto a pedali: la Hummer. In un catalogo della americana Butler Brothers del 1914 è descritta con sedile regolabile, sterzo, colori rosso e verde. Con ruote gommate costava 3,15 dollari.

One of the oldest types of pedal-car: the Hummer. In a 1914 catalogue from the American Butler Brothers, it was described as having adjustable seats, steering wheel and red and green as colours. It cost 3.15 dollars with rubber wheels.

Une des premières voitures à pédales: la Hummer. Dans un catalogue de la firme américaine Butler Brothers de 1914, elle est décrite avec un siège réglable, un volant et une carrosserie rouge ou verte. Elle coûtait 3,15 dollars avec des roues à bandage de caoutchouc.

Eines der ältesten Tretautos: der Hummer. In einem Katalog der amerikanischen Firma Butler Brothers von 1914 wird er mit verstellbarem Sitz, Lenkung und roter und grüner Farbe beschrieben. Mit Gummirädern, kostete er 3,15 Dollar.

Così erano fatte le vetturette per bambini ai primi anni del secolo: costruite artigianalmente, avevano carrozzeria in legno, ruote in ferro e meccanica molto semplice ripresa dai velocipedi. Questo modello, di origine sconosciuta, si fa risalire al 1905.

This is how children's cars were made in the first years of this century: built by craftsmen, they had wooden bodies, iron wheels and very simple mechanics adapted from the tricycle. This particular model, of unknown origin, goes back to about 1905.

Voilà comment étaient fabriquées les autos pour enfants au début du siècle; réalisation artisanale, carrosserie en bois, roues en fer et mécanique très simple reprise des vélos. Ce modèle, d'origine inconnue, remonte aux années 1905.

So sahem die Kinderautos in den ersten Jahren unseres Jahrhunderts aus: in Handwerksbetrieben hergestellt, hatten sie eine Holzkarosserie, Eisenräder und die sehr einfache von den Fahrrädern übernommene Mechanik. Dieses Modell unbekannten Ursprungs stammt wohl aus dem Jahr 1905.

Francia, inizio secolo: un classico esempio di auto a pedali prima maniera con ruote in ferro di tipo ciclistico, carrozzeria in legno, sterzo a cremagliera, trasmissione a catena.

France, early this century: a classic example of a pedal-car in the early style with cycle-type iron wheels, a wooden body, a rack steering wheel and block chain drive.

France, début du siècle: un exemple classique d'auto à pédales première manière, avec roues en fer de type cycliste, carrosserie en bois, dirction à crémaillère et transmission par chaîne.

Frankreich, Jahrhundertbeginn: klassisches Beispiel eines Tretautos in der ersten Machart mit Eisenrädern im Fahrradstil, Holzkarosserie, Zahnstangenlenkung, Kettenübertragung.

Una deliziosa vetturetta costruita in Austria ai tempi dell'Imperatore Francesco Giuseppe: reca una targa in cui è riprodotto il nome del negozio Josef Muhbanse, fornitore della Casa imperiale austriaca.

A delightful model car made in Austria in the time of Emperor Franz Joseph: the licence plate bears the name of Josef Muhbanse, supplier to the Imperial Court of Austria.

Une délicieuse petite auto réalisée en Autriche au temps de l'empereur François-Joseph. Sa plaquette porte le nom de Josef Muhbanse, fournisseur officiel de la Maison Impériale d'Autriche.

Ein köstliches in Österreich zur Keit Kaisers Franz Joseph gebautes Kinderauto: trägt ein Schild mit dem Namen des Geschäfts: Josef Muhbanse, k. u. k. Hoflieferant.

41

Le prime auto a pedali erano per lo più giocattoli molto semplici, un po' rozzi di fattura, quasi sempre in legno e con ruote a raggi. Questa arieggia una Renault dei primi del Novecento; carrozzeria in legno, trasmissione a catena, lunghezza m. 1,20.

The first pedal-cars were for the most part very simple, quite roughly made, almost always of wood with spoked wheels. This one copies a Renault of the early 1900s, has a wooden body, block chain drive and is 1.20 metres long.

Les premières autos à pédales étaient avant tout des jouets très simples, à la facture spartiate, presque toujours en bois avec des roues à rayons. Celle-ci évoque une Renault du début du siècle, avec sa carrosserie en bois, sa transmission par chaîne, pour une longueur de 1,20 m.

Die ersten Tretautos waren meistens sehr einfache Spielsachen, etwas roh in der Ausführung, fast immer aus Holz mit Speichenrädern. Das abgebildete Autochen inspiriert sich an einem Renault der ersten Jahre unseres Jahrhunderts; Holzkarosserie, Kettenübertragung, Länge 1,20 m.

Questa graziosa riproduzione della Vauxhall Prince Henry 1914 venne costruita nel 1915 per il figlio dell'ingegner Pomeroy. La medesima vetturetta appare nella copertina accanto alla vettura vera.

This attractive reproduction of the Vauxhall Prince Henry 1914 was built in 1915 for the son of the engineer Pomeroy. The same model appears on the cover next to the real car.

Cette jolie reproduction de la Vauxhall Prince Henry de 1914 fut réalisée en 1915 pour le fils de l'ingénieur Pomeroy. C'est la même auto qui figure sur la couverture à côté du modèle original grandeur nature.

Diese anmutige Nachbildung des Vauxhall Prince Henry 1914 wurde 1915 für den Sohn des Ingenieurs Pomeroy gebaut. Dasselbe Autochen erscheint auf der Titelseite neben dem echten Wagen.

Non si può dire bella, ma ha un suo fascino questa vetturetta a pedali in legno e metallo degli anni venti: è lunga m. 1,60 e dispone di due posti più un terzo di fortuna ricavato dal baule posteriore.

It could hardly be called beautiful, but this twenties' wood and metal pedal-car still has its charm. It is 1.60 metres long, has two seats plus a dicky seat that was stored away in the trunk at the back.

Sans être belle, on ne peut pas dire que cette auto à pédales manque de charme. Réalisée dans les années vingt en bois et en métal, elle mesure 1,60 m de long et en plus des deux places à l'avant, elle en offre une troisième de secours aménagée dans la malle arrière.

Man kann es zwar nicht als schön bezeichnen, aber dieses Tretautochen aus Holz und Metall besitzt einen ganz eigenen Charme: es ist 1,60 m lang und verfügt über zwei Sitzplätze, sowie einen aus dem hinteren Kofferraum gewonnenen Notsitz.

La "Baby" Bugatti Grand Prix tipo "52". Costruita da Ettore Bugatti per il figlio Roland, entrò in produzione nel 1930 e venne realizzata in soli 90 esemplari. Motore elettrico, freni a tamburo, peso 70 kg, lunghezza m. 1,85, velocità 15 km/h. Questo esemplare fu donato dalla Famiglia Agnelli al Museo dell'Automobile di Torino.

The "Baby" Bugatti Grand Prix "52". Built by Ettore Bugatti for his son Roland, it went into production in 1930; only 90 models were made. It had an electric motor, drum brakes, weighed 70 kg, was 1.85 metres long and went at 15 kmph. This particular model was given by the Agnelli family to the Museo dell'Automobile of Turin.

"La "Baby" Bugatti Grand Prix type "52". Construite par Ettore Bugatti pour son fils Roland, elle entra en production en 1930 et fut réalisée à 90 exemplaires seulement. Moteur électrique, freins à tambour, poids 70 kg, longueur 1,85 m, vitesse 15 km/h. Cet exemplaire a été donné par la famille Agnelli au Musée de l'Automobile de Turin.

Der "Baby" Bugatti Grand Prix Typ "52": Von Ettore Bugatti für seinen Sohn Roland gebaut, wurde seine Produktion 1930 aufgenommen, allerdings wurden nur 90 Exemplare hergestellt. Elektromotor, Trommelbremsen, Gewicht 70 kg, Länge 1,85 m, Höchstgeschwindigkeit 15 km/std. Dieses Exemplar wurde von der Familie Agnelli dem Automobilmuseum von Turin geschenkt.

"Vetturetta del Comm. Cella o vetturetta per ragazzi tipo ABC": con questo nome Guido Cattaneo dell'Isotta Fraschini ideò nel 1928 una vetturetta altamente sofisticata per i figli dell'amministratore della Società. Provvista di motore a 4 cilindri della Peugeot "5CV", la vetturetta ABC venne costruita in due soli esemplari, uno dei quali, modificato da Trossi, è oggi conservato al Museo dell'Automobile di Torino.

"Commendatore Cella's model car or model car for children type ABC". It was in 1928 that Guido Cattaneo of Isotta Fraschini conceived the highly sophisticated car of this name, to be presented to the sons of the manager of the company. Provided with a 4 cylinder Peugeot "5CV" engine, only two models of the ABC were built, one of which, modified by Trossi, is now preserved in the Museo dell'Automobile in Turin.

"Voiturette du Comm. Cella ou voiturette pour enfants type ABC": c'est le nom que Guido Cattaneo d'Isotta Fraschini a donné à ce modèle hautement sophistiqué mis au point en 1928 pour les enfants de l'administrateur de la société. Equipée d'un moteur 4 cylindres de la Peugeot "5 CV", le modèle "ABC" ne fut réalisé qu'en deux exemplaires, dont un modifié par Trossi est aujourd'hui conservé au Musée de l'Automobile de Turin.

"Kinderauto des Comm. Cella oder Kinderauto Typ ABC": Unter dieser Benennung schuf Guido Cattaneo von der Firma Isotta Fraschini 1928 ein höchst ausgeklügeltes Autochen für die Kinder des Geschäftsführers der Gesellschaft. Mit dem Vierzylindermotor des Peugeot "5CV" ausgestattet, wurde das Autochen ABC nur in zwei Exemplaren gebaut; eines von ihnen, von Trossi umgebaut, wird heute in Automobilmuseum von Turin aufbewahrt.

Fra il 1924 e il 1930 la Bentley conseguì ben cinque vittorie al circuito di Le Mans. Particolarmente significativa l'affermazione del 1929 con quattro "4,1/2 lit." ai primi posti. Ecco una splendida riproduzione per bambini opera di M. Phillips: ha motore elettrico e pneumatici in gomma.

Between 1924 and 1930 Bentley achieved a good five victories on the circuit at Le Mans. Particularly significant was their performance in 1929 when four "4 1/2 lit"s took the first places. Here is a splendid reproduction for children made by M. Phillips: it has an electric motor and rubber tyres.

De 1924 à 1930, Bentley remporta cinq victoires au Mans avec, en 1929 un record exceptionnel: quatre Bentley "4 1/2 lit" aux premières places. Voici une splendide reproduction pour enfants équipée d'un moteur électrique et de pneus. Elle est l'œuvre de M. Phillips.

Zwischen 1924 und 1930 errang der Bentley fünf Siege auf dem Ring von Le Mans. Von besonderer Bedeutung war der Sieg von 1929 mit vier "Viereinhalbliter" - Rennwagen auf den ersten Plätzen. Hier ist eine großartige Nachbildung für Kinder, von M. Phillips ausgeführt: das Rennautochen hat einen Elektromotor und Gummireifen.

Tre piccole Packard prodotte negli Stati Uniti dalla American National Company. In alto a sinistra una vetturetta a pedali del 1931 restaurata recentemente da George Tissen. Sotto: vetturetta con motore elettrico del 1928. Qui sopra, un delizioso coupé per bambini del 1925.

Three small Packards made in the U.S.A. by the American National Company. Top left, a 1931 toy pedal car recently restored by George Tissen. Below, a 1928 model car with electric motor. Above, a delightful coupé for children built in 1925.

Trois petites Packard produites aux Etats Unis par American National Company. En haut à gauche, une voiture à pédales de 1931 récemment restaurée par George Tissen. En bas: une auto junior à moteur électrique de 1928. En haut, un délicieux coupé pour enfants de 1925.

Drei kleine, in den Vereinigten Staaten von der American National Company hergestellte Packards. Obenlinks ein Kleine Tretauto von 1931, das vor kurzem von George Tissen restauriert wurde. Unten: ein Wägelchen mit Elektromotor von 1928. Gleich oben, ein anmutiges Kindercoupé von 1925.

NUOVA FABBRICA DI CARROZZINE DA PASSEGGIO - TRICICLI E GIOCATTOLI PER BIMBI
Ditta P. GIORDANI :: BOLOGNA - VIALE FORO BOARIO, N. 38

AUTOMOBILE A PEDALE
PER BIMBI - A DUE POSTI

Articolo di costruzione identica al precedente Num. 6, però a due posti e doppio movimento .. .. L. 45,—

Con ruote rivestite di gomma, in più .. 10,50

FIG. N. 7

Auto per bimbi "Tipo popolare"

Verniciato a smalto con colori vivaci, elegante imbottitura, ruote con gomme smontabili a sistema brevettato, volante automaticamente abbassabile a sistema brevettato.

lunghezza totale cm. 100 - ruote diametro cm. 28   Prezzo Numero unico L.

Auto a due posti

	N. 1	N. 2
DIAMETRO delle ruote . . . . . cm.	20	25
LUNGHEZZA totale . . . . »	137	147

CARROZZERIA in lamiera stampata.
VERNICIATURA brillantissima.
PEDALIERE anteriore e posteriore.

Auto corsa lusso N. 2 con pneumatici

Vedi caratteristiche dell'auto corsa lusso N. 2.
RUOTE pneumatiche del diametro di cm. 32.
Si può fornire anche con sirena.

Auto spider lusso

	N. 1	N. 2
DIAMETRO delle ruote . . . . . cm.	20	25
LUNGHEZZA totale . . . . »	93	116

CARROZZERIA in lamiera stampata.
VERNICIATURA alla nitro cellulosa.
RUOTE a disco con gomma.
PARAFANGHI e pedane in lamiera stampata.
IMPIANTO ELETTRICO di illuminazione.
TROMBA - Paraurti - Parabrise - Indicatore di direzione - Targa.

AUTO "ROMA" NORMALE N. 2
LINEA AERODINAMICA MODERNISSIMA IN LAMIERA STAMPATA

DIAMETRO DELLE RUOTE CM. 26
LUNGHEZZA TOTALE CM. 120

Movimento a catena, con rapporto di velocità.

Ruote in lamiera stampata, con cappellotti nichelati e gomme mm. 13.

Radiatore speciale tipo corsa.

Verniciatura brillantissima a due colori.

Adatto per bambini da 4-7 anni.

Auto gran lusso (2 posti)

Ditta RAFFAELE GIORDANI
BOLOGNA - Via Nicolò Dall'Arca 52
Telefono 27-039

Diametro delle ruote . . . . . cm. 30
Lunghezza totale . . . . " 140

UGUALE nelle caratteristiche generali al precedente
AUTO GRAN LUSSO ad 1 posto

Rinforzato nella intelaiatura per renderlo adatto al maggior peso da trasportare

AUTO SPIDER Tipo LUSSO

Ditta RAFFAELE GIORDANI
BOLOGNA - Via Nicolò Dall'Arca 52
Telefono 27-039

Diametro delle ruote . . . . . cm. 25
Lunghezza totale . . . . " 125

Carrozzeria in lamiera stampata
Verniciatura alla nitrocellulosa
Ruote a disco con gomme
Parafanghi e Pedane in lamiera stampata
Impianto elettrico d'illuminazione, funzionante

Tromba - Paraurti - Parabrise - Indicatore di direzione - Targa

Solidità massima - Linea elegantissima

Tratti da cataloghi Giordani di varie epoche, ecco alcuni fra i modelli più rappresentativi prodotti dalla Casa italiana fra il 1915 e il 1935. La Giordani costruiva tricicli per bambini già nel 1895.

Here, taken from Giordani catalogues of various years, are some of the most representative models produced by the Italian firm between 1915 and 1935. Giordani was already making tricycles for children in 1895.

Tirés des catalogues Giordani de différentes époques, voici quelques-uns des modèles les plus représentatifs de la firme italienne de 1915 à 1935. Giordani fabriquait des tricycles pour enfants en 1895 déjà.

Aus den Katalogen der Firma Giordani aus verschiedenen Epochen ausgewählt, zeigen wir hier einige der typischsten Modelle, die von der italienischen Firma zwischen 1915 und 1935 hergestellt wurden. Die Firma Giordani baute schon 1895 Kinderdreiräder.

Italia, 1926: questa auto per bambini tipo "corsa" con la caratteristica coda a punta era prodotta dalla Giordani. La carrozzeria era in lamiera verniciata a smalto, le ruote smontabili e il volante regolabile a misura del bambino.

Italy 1926: this "racing" car for children with the characteristic pointed tail was made by Giordani. The body was made of metal and finished in enamel, the wheels could be removed and the steering wheel adjusted to suit the child.

Italie, 1926: ce modèle type course avec l'arrière caractéristique en pointe était produit par Giordani. La carrosserie était en tôle vernie à l'émail, les roues pouvaient être déposées et le volant se réglait selon l'âge de l'enfant.

Italien 1926: dieser "Rennwagen" für Kinder mit dem typischen Spitzheck wurde von der Firma Giordani hergestellt. Die Karosserie war aus lackiertem Bleck, die Räder konnten abmontiert und das Lenkrad je nach Größe des Kindes eingestellt werden.

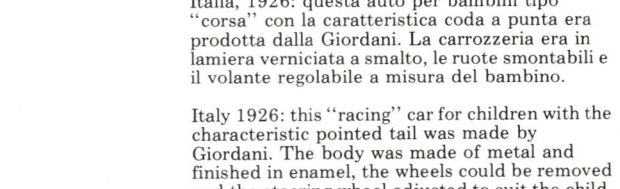

"Five-Ton Mack dump truck": con questo nome era definito un camioncino per bambini prodotto nel 1925 dalla Casa americana Steelcraft e provvisto del cassone ribaltabile.

"Five-Ton Mack dump truck": this was the name given to this small lorry for children which was made in 1925 by the American company Steelcraft and provided with a tip-up container.

"Five-Ton Mack dump truck": c'est le nom de ce camion pour enfants produit en 1925 par la firme américaine Steelcraft et équipé d'une benne basculante.

"Five-Ton Mack dump truck": diesen Namen trug ein kleiner Kinder-Lastwagen, der 1925 von der amerikanischen Firma Steelcraft produziert wurde und der mit einem Kippkasten ausgestattet war.

Una pagina pubblicitaria della Casa americana Sidway, che presenta una vetturetta a pedali e reclamizza la produzione di auto, velocipedi e carretti. L'inserzione è dell'agosto del 1929.

A page of publicity from the American firm Sidway, showing a pedal car and advertising their line of cars, cycles and carts. The advertisement appeared in August 1929.

Une page publicitaire de la firme américaine Sidway qui présente une auto à pédales et réclamise sa production d'autos, de vélos et de charrettes. L'annonce porte la date de 1929.

Eine Werbeanzeige der amerikanischen Firma Sidway, die ein Tretauto vorstellt und Reklame für die Herstellung von Autos, Fahrrädern und Schubkarren macht. Die Anzeige stammt vom August 1929.

Una divertente inserzione pubblicitaria del 1925: la Steelcraft americana reclamizza per Natale le sue vetturette per bambini, che costano da 15 dollari in su.

An amusing advertisement of 1925: the American Steelcraft is advertising its children's cars for Christmas. They cost from 15 dollars.

Une amusante annonce publicitaire de 1925: la maison américaine Steelcraft réclamise pour Noël ses autos pour enfants; prix à partir de 15 dollars.

Eine amüsante Werbeanzeige von 1925: die amerikanische Firma Steelcraft wirbt zu Weihnachten für ihre Kinderautos, die ab 15 Dollars aufwärts zu kaufen sind.

Una vetturetta di fabbricazione italiana che ricorda la Fiat "509" del 1925. La carrozzeria in legno è ricoperta, come nella Weymann, in finta pelle, dispone di due posti e reca sulla cornice del radiatore il marchio Fiat.

A model car made in Italy which recalls the Fiat "509" of 1925. The body was made of wood and was covered, like the Weymann, in imitation leather. It has two seats and bears on the radiator the name Fiat.

Une voiturette de fabrication italienne qui rappelle la Fiat "509" de 1925. La carrosserie est en bois revêtu de similicuir, comme la Weymann. Elle offre deux places et porte la marque Fiat sur le radiateur.

Ein Kinderauto italienischer Herstellung, das an den Fiat "509" von 1925 erinnert. Die Holzkarosserie ist wie bei Weymann mit Kunstleder verkleidet; das Autochen verfügt über zwei Sitzplätze und trägt auf der Kühlerblende das Markenzeichen Fiat.

Inghilterra, 1930: una vetturetta a pedali con ruote in ferro e capottina ripiegabile prodotta dalla Triang, la più prolifica marca inglese in questo settore.

England 1930: a pedal-car with iron wheels and a soft top made by Triang, the biggest English producers of pedal-cars.

Grande Bretagne, 1930: une auto à pédales avec roues métalliques et capote rabattable, produite par Triang le constructeur anglais le plus actif dans ce secteur.

England 1930: ein Tretauto mit Eisenrädern und Faltverdeck von der Firma Triang, der in dieser Branche produktivsten englischen Marke.

Dall'album di famiglia degli anni venti. Prima foto: una vetturetta da corsa con la caratteristica coda a punta fotografata in Inghilterra. Seconda: il piccolo Bruno nella sua auto a pedali, Italia 1929. Terza: un bébé inglese al volante della sua spider.

From a family album of the twenties. First photo: a racing car for children with the characteristic pointed tail photographed in England. Second: the young Bruno in his pedal-car, Italy 1929. Third: an English child at the wheel of his spider.

Tiré de l'album de famille des années vingt. Première photo: une auto de course avec son arrière pointu photographiée en Grande Bretagne. Deuxième: le petit Bruno dans son auto à pédales, Italie 1929. Troisième: un petit anglais au volant de son spider.

Aus einem Familienalbum der Zwanzigerjahre. Erstes Foto: ein Mini-Rennauto mit dem typischen Spitzheck, in England aufgenommen.
Zweite Aufnahme: der kleine Bruno in seinem Tretauto, Italien 1929.
Dritte Aufnahme: ein englisches Baby am Steuer seines Spiders.

61

Un giovanissimo pilota, al volante di una Bugatti "Baby" tipo "52" elettrica, impegnato allo spasimo in una delle tante gare organizzate in Francia con le celebri vetturette, attorno al 1930.

A very young driver at the wheel of an electric "Baby" Bugatti type "52", doing his hardest in one of the many competitions organised in France with these famous cars around 1930.

Un tout jeune pilote au volant d'une Bugatti "Baby" type "52" électrique engagé à fond dans une des nombreuses courses pour autos juniors organisées en France vers 1930.

Ein blutjunger Rennfahrer am Steuer eines Bugatti "Baby" vom Typ "52" mit Elektroantrieb. Er gibt alles in einer jener zahlreichen Wettfahrten, die in Frankreich um 1930 mit den berühmten Mini-Rennwagen durchgeführt wurden.

Ancora le famose Bugattine in azione: questa foto venne scattata a Barcellonette in Francia in occasione di un Grand Prix delle "Baby" patrocinato dal rappresentante della Bugatti a Nizza, M. Ernest Friderich.

The famous little Bugattis once again in action: this photo was taken at Barcellonette in France on the occasion of the Babies' Grand Prix, sponsored by the Bugatti representative in Nice, Mr. Ernest Friderich.

Toujours les fameuses Bugatti en action: cette photo a été prise en France, à Barcellonette, à l'occasion d'un Grand Prix des "Baby" organisé par la représentant Bugatti de Nice M. Ernest Friderich.

Noch einmal die berühmten Mini-Bugattis in Aktion: dieses Foto wurde in Barcellonette in Frankreich anläßlich eines Grand Prix für Kinderrennautos aufgenommen, das unter der Schirmherrschaft des Vertreters der Firma Bugatti in Nizza, Herrn Ernest Friderich, abgehalten wurde.

Un gruppo di auto a pedali degli anni trenta. In alto a sinistra una "Ardita" in legno che prende il nome da una Fiat del tempo; a destra una vetturetta da corsa in metallo Laura-Candelo; sotto un modello aerodinamico del 1939 della Triang inglese.

A group of pedal-cars from the thirties. At the top on the left is a wooden "Ardita", the name of which comes from a Fiat of the time; on the right is a Laura-Candelo metal racing car; underneath is a 1939 aerodynamic model from the English Triang.

Un groupe d'autos à pédales des années trente. En haut à gauche une "Ardita" en bois qui prend son nom d'une Fiat de l'époque; à droite, une auto de course métallique de Laura-Candelo; en bas, un modèle aérodynamique de 1939 de la firme anglaise Triang.

Eine Gruppe von Tretautos der Dreißigerjahre, Oben links ein "Ardita" aus Holz, der seinen Namen von einem Fiat der damaligen Zeit übernommen hat; rechts ein Rennwägelchen aus Metall Laura-Candelo; unten ein windschnittiges Modell der englischen Firma Triang von 1939.

Questa vetturetta, fabbricata in Inghilterra verso il 1938 dalla Triang ha una linea piuttosto austera: potrebbe nascondere una lontana parentela con una Rover dell'epoca.

This model car, made in England in about 1938 by Triang is fairly austere in shape; there could be a distant relationship with a Rover of the time.

Cette petite auto réalisée par Triang en 1938 a une ligne plutôt austère: elle pourrait être apparentée avec une Rover de l'époque.

Dieses von der Firma Triang um 1938 hergestelltes Kinderauto hat eine ziemlich strenge Linienführung: man könnte eine gewisse entfernte Verwandtschaft mit einem damaligen Rover feststellen.

Un'altra bella vetturetta per bambini della inesauribile Triang inglese, alla quale si deve una infinità di modelli specie nell'anteguerra. Questa riproduce una Packard della seconda metà degli anni trenta.

Another fine car for children from Triang's unending resources: they produced an infinite number of models especially before the war. This is a reproduction of a Packard, from the late thirties.

Une autre belle auto pour enfants de l'inépuisable Triang, constructeur anglais auquel on doit une infinité de modèles surtout avant la deuxième guerre mondiale. Celle-ci reproduit une Packard vers la deuxième moitié des années trente.

Ein weiteres schönes Kinderautochen der unerschöpflichen englischen Firma Triang, der man eine unendliche Reihe von Modellen besonders in der Vorkriegszeit verdankt. Das gezeigte Modell stellt einen Packard dar, und zwar aus der zweiten Hälfte der Dreißiger Jahre.

Radiatore con le tipiche scanalature ed emblema Vauxhall, pneumatici in gomma, luci, parti in legno e metallo, parabrezza inclinabile, tanica di scorta, sospensioni, tromba: era questa la più cara vetturetta a pedali che figurava nel catalogo Triang del 1932.

This was the most expensive pedal model that appeared in the Triang catalogue of 1932. It had a radiator with the typical grooves and Vauxhall emblem, rubber tyres, parts in wood and metal, sloping windscreen, reserve tank, suspension and a horn.

Radiateur portant les cannelures typiques et l'emblème de Vauxhall, pneus en gomme, pièces en bois et en métal, pare-brise rabattable, jerrycan de réserve, suspensions et klaxon: c'était l'auto à pédales la plus chère du catalogue Triang de 1932.

Ein Kühler mit den typischen Rillen und dem Emblem des Vauxhall, mit Gummireifen, Scheinwerfern, Holz- und Metallteilen, neigbarer Windschutzscheibe, Ersatzkanister, Federung und Hupe: dies ist das teuerste Tretauto im Katalog der Firma Triang von 1932.

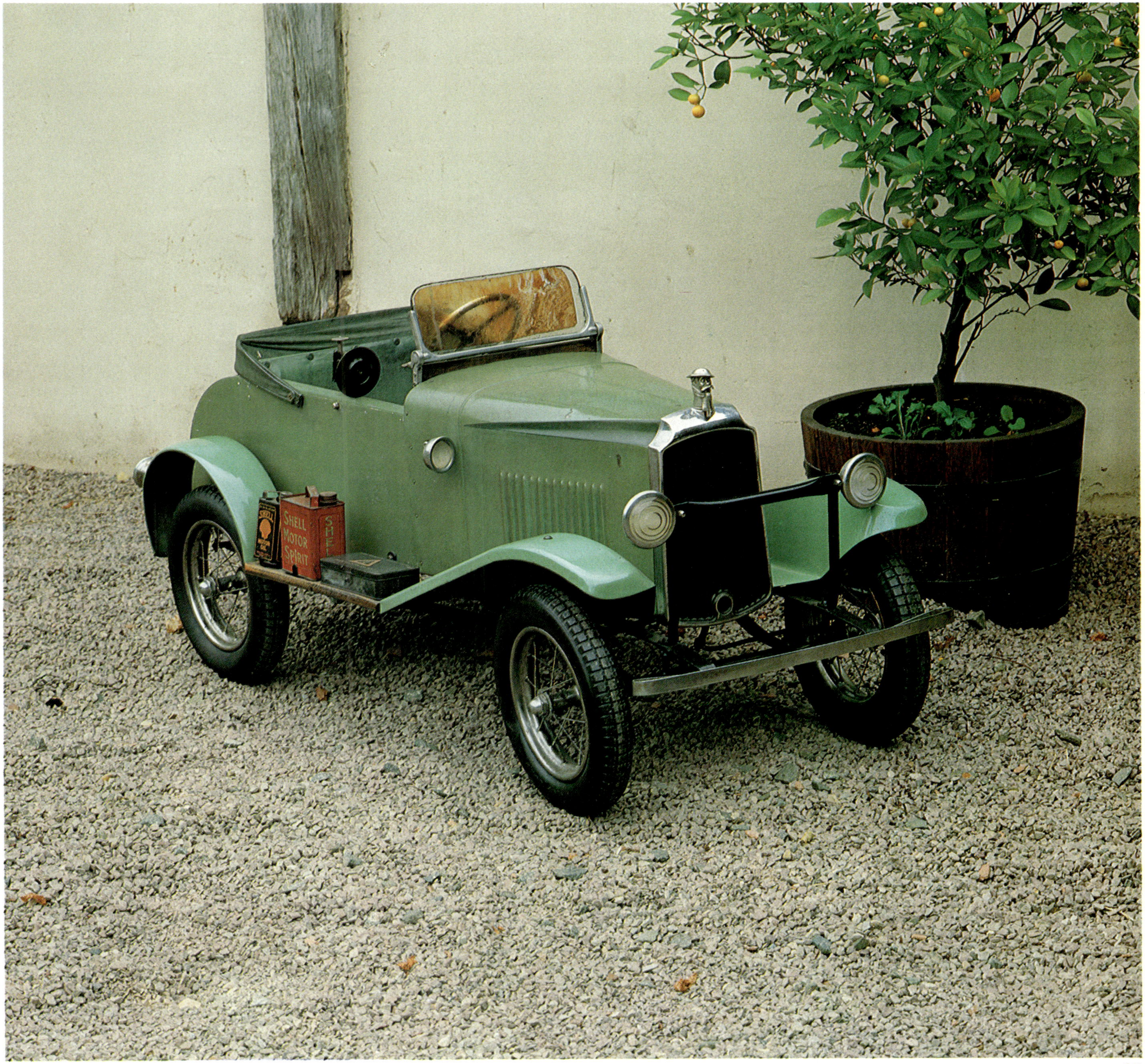
SHELL MOTOR SPIRIT

Ardita: questa piccola automobile a pedali con carrozzeria in legno fabbricata in Italia prima della guerra porta sul radiatore il nome di una elegante vettura della Fiat degli anni trenta, nota anche come "518".

Ardita: this small pedal-car with a wooden body, made in Italy before the war, carries on the radiator the name of an elegant Fiat car of the thirties, also known as "518".

Ardita: cette petite auto à pédales avec carrosserie en bois était fabriquée en Italie avant la deuxième guerre mondiale. Sur le radiateur, le nom d'une élégante voiture Fiat des années trente, connue aussi come "518".

Ardita. Dieses kleine, in Italien vor dem Krieg hergestellte Tretauto mit Holzkarosserie trägt auf dem Kühler den Namen eines eleganten Fiatwagens der Dreißigerjahre, bekannt auch als "518".

Nel 1938 la Lines Bros Triang produceva questa vetturetta a pedali in legno e metallo che, particolarmente nel radiatore, aveva le sembianze di una Daimler. Con pneumatici gonfiabili costava 7,49 sterline; a gomma piena 5 sterline.

In 1938 Lines Bros Triang produced this pedal-car, made of wood and metal, of which the radiator in particular resembled a Daimler. With inflatable tyres, it cost £ 7.49 sterling; with solid rubber ones £ 5 sterling.

C'est en 1938 que la Lines Bros Triang produisit cette auto à pédales en bois et métal dont la ligne, et plus particulièrement le radiateur, rappelle la Daimler de l'époque. Equipée de pneus pleins, elle coûtait 5 livres sterlings, et 7,49 avec des pneus gonflables.

1938 stellte die Lines Bros Triang dieses Tretauto aus Holz und Metall her, das besonders in der Kühlerpartie einem Daimler ähnelte. Mit aufblasbaren Gummireifen kostete es 7,49 Pfund, mit Vollgummireifen 5 Pfund.

Anche le auto a pedali seguono la moda: le tendenze aerodinamiche degli anni trenta trovano un esempio in questa "Teddy Airline" prodotta in Inghilterra verso il 1938, la cui linea si rifà alla caposcuola Airflow.

Even pedal-car followed fashion: the aerodynamic tendencies from the thirties reveal themselves in this "Teddy Airline" made in England in around 1938, the shape of which has strong links with the leading Airflow.

Les autos à pédales aussi suivent la mode: les tendances aérodynamiques des années trente se retrouvent dans cette "Teddy Airline" réalisée en Grande Bretagne vers 1938. Sa ligne descend en droite ligne de la Airflow, chef de file.

Auch Tretautos folgen der Mode: die windschnittigen Neigungen der Dreißigerjahre fanden ein Beispiel in diesem "Teddy Airline", der in England um 1938 hergestellt wurde und der sich in der Linienführung an dem wichtigsten Vertreter Airflow inspirierte.

Una delle prime auto per bambini del dopoguerra: la Austin "twin cam". La fabbricava già nel 1949 la Austin Junior Car Factory, un apposito stabilimento sorto a Pengam nel Nuovo Galles, dove lavorava un gruppo di ex minatori invalidi.

One of the firs post-war cars for children: the Austin "twin cam". It was already being produced in 1949 by the Austin Junior Car Factory, a factory especially set up for this line of production at Pengam in Wales, the labour force of which was a group of disabled ex-miners.

Une des premières autos pour enfants de l'après-guerre: l'Austin "twin cam". Dans le 1949, le constructeur était déjà la Austin Junior Car Factory qui avait créé expressément un atelier à Pengam dans le Pays de Galles, où travaillait un groupe d'anciens mineurs invalides.

Eines der ersten Kinderautos der Nachkriegszeit: der Austin "twin cam". Er wurde schon 1949 von der Austin Junior Car Factory, einer extra dafür in Pengam in Neu Wales gegründeten Fabrik, in der eine Gruppe von kriegsinvaliden Bergarbeitern arbeitete, hergestellt.

Una splendida riproduzione della Cisitalia Grand Prix per bambini realizzata a Torino nel 1952 da Piero Patria. Motore di 75 cc., cambio a tre velocità, sospensioni sulle 4 ruote. Lunghezza m. 2,35, peso 104 kg., velocità 70 km/h. Al volante è il figlio del costruttore Franco, che, divenuto poi corridore, perì in un incidente a Montlhéry nel 1964.

A splendi reproduction for children of the Cisitalia Grand Prix, made by Piero Patria at Turin in 1952. 75 cc engine, three gears, four wheel suspension. Lenght 2.35 m, weight 104 kg, speed 70 kmph. At the wheel is the maker's son Franco, who was to become a racing driver and died in an accident at Montlhéry in 1964.

Une splendide reproduction de la Cisitalia Grand Prix pour enfants réalisée à Turin par Piero Patria en 1952. Moteur de 75 cm³, boîte à trois rapports, suspensions sur les 4 roues. Longueur 2,35 m., poids 104 kg, vitesse 70 km/h. Au volant, Franco le fils du constructeur. Devenu coureur automobile, il mourra dans un accident en 1964 à Montlhéry.

Eine großartige Reproduktion des Cisitalia Grand Prix für Kinder, 1952 in Turin von Piero Patria ausgeführt. Motor mit 75 ccm Hubraum, Dreiganschaltung, Vierradfederung, Länge 2,35 m, Gewicht 104 kg, Höchstgeschwindigkeit 70 km/std. Am Steuer der Sohn des Konstrukteurs, der später Rennfahrer wurde und 1964 in Montlhéry tödlich verunglückte.

Francia, 1931: ben undici Bugatti "Baby" tipo "52" con motore elettrico sono allineate al traguardo di una gara riservata ai bambini che si disputava allo Stadio Buffalo di Parigi. Sotto: il rituale mazzo di fiori offerto al vincitore della gara.

France, 1931: eleven "Baby" Bugatti type "52" with electric motors at the finishing line of a race for children only at the Buffalo Stadium in Paris. Below, the customary bunch of flowers given to the winner of the race.

France, 1931: onze Bugatti "Baby" type "52" à moteur électrique sont alignées au départ d'une course réservée aux enfants qui se disputait au strade Buffalo de Paris. Dessous, le rituel bouquet de fleurs offert au vainqueur de la course.

Frankreich 1931: gut 11 Bugatti Baby vom Typ "52" mit Elektromotor stehen am Start eines Kindern vorbehaltenen Rennens aufgereiht, das im Stadion Buffalo von Paris abgehalten wurde. Unten: der traditionelle, dem Sieger des Rennens dargereichte Blumenstrauß.

Il piccolo Luigi, posato il cappello alla marinara sul cofano, pare molto soddisfatto della sua vetturetta, una Giordani degli anni trenta.

Little Luigi, with his sailor hat on the bonnet, looks very satisfied with his model car, a Giordani of the thirties.

Le petit Luigi, son béret de marin sur le coffre, semble très satisfait de sa voiture, une Giordani des années trente.

Der kleine Luigi hat seine Matrosenmütze auf die Kühlerhaube gelegt; mit seinem Autochen, einem Giordani der Dreißigerjahre, scheint er sehr zufrieden zu sein.

Avevano il classico radiatore Bugatti, la tinta azzurra e le ruote a disco cerchiate in gomma queste vetturette prodotte dalla famosa marca francese Eureka. La foto è del 1934.

These cars, examples of the famous French Eureka models, had the classic Bugatti radiator, solid wheels with rubber tyres, and were blue in colour. The photo was taken in 1934.

Ces autos produites par le célèbre constructeur français Euréka montaient le classique radiateur Bugatti, des roues à flasques avec bandage en caoutchouc sur une carrosserie bleue. La photo est datée 1934.

Diese von der französischen Firma Eureka hergestellten Kinderautos besaßen die klassische Kühlerhaube von Bugatti, waren blau gelackt und hatten Scheibenräder mit Gummireifen. Das Foto stammt aus dem Jahre 1934.

Una inserzione pubblicitaria del 1930: la Ditta Bolzani e Grimoldi di Milano, fabbrica di carrozzelle e tricicli fondata nel 1904, reclamizza una sua vetturetta a pedali con trasmissione a catena.

An advertisement of 1930: the firm Bolzani and Grimoldi of Milan, makers of baby carriages and tricycles founded in 1904, is advertising one of their pedal-cars with block chain drive.

Une annonce publicitaire de 1930: la maison Bolzani e Grimoldi de Milan, fabrique de landaus et de tricycles fondée en 1904, réclame une de ses autos à pédales avec transmission par chaîne.

Eine Werbeanzeige von 1930: die 1904 gegründete Kinderwagen- und Dreiradfabrik Bolzani e Grimoldi aus Mailand wirbt für ein Tretauto mit Kettenantrieb.

Ditta BOLZÀNI GRIMOLDI & C. - Milano [123] Via C. Balbo, 9 Telefono 51 212
DI EUGENIO GRIMOLDI (CASA FONDATA NEL 1904)
Premiata Fabbrica Lombarda di Carrozzelle per Bambini · Bambole ed Infermi, Tricicli, ecc.

Charrettes
Sedie trasformabili per bambini
Commissioni - Riparazioni

Medaglia d'oro
Camera di Comm. di Milano

CATALOGHI E PREVENTIVI GRATIS A RICHIESTA

Prima della partenza un giovane pilota con tanto di cuffia, occhiali e tuta da corridore, sta controllando, a cofano aperto, la sua vetturetta a pedali, una Chenard et Walcker del 1933.

Before driving off, a young driver fitted out with ear muffs, goggles and driver's overalls is checking his pedal-car with the bonnet open. The car is a Chenard et Walcker of 1933.

Avant de prendre le départ, un jeune pilote casqué, avec lunettes et combinaison de coureur, contrôle - coffre ouvert - son auto à pédales, une Chenard et Walcker de 1933.

Vor der Abfahrt kontrolliert ein junger Fahrer mit großem Sturzhelm, Rennbrille und Rennanzug sein Tretauto, einen Chenard et Walcker von 1933. Die Motorhaube steht natürlich offen.

Chiaramente ispirata ad una Rolls Royce "Twenty", questa vetturetta risale al 1930 e venne prodotta dalla Triang inglese. Azionata da motore elettrico, aveva sportelli e cofano apribili. Ad un'asta inglese del 1973 venne aggiudicata per 700 sterline.

Clearly inspired by a Rolls Royce "Twenty", this model car goes back to 1930 and was made by the English Triang. Operated by an electric motor, it had doors and a bonnet which could be opened. In England in 1973 it fetched £ 700 at auction.

Produite par Triang en Grande Bretagne, cette auto remonte à 1930 et s'inspire clairement de la Rolls Royce "Twenty". Elle était actionnée par un moteur électrique. Le coffre et les portières s'ouvraient. A une vente aux enchères anglaise en 1973, cet exemplaire a été adjugé pour 700 livres sterlings.

In klarer Anlehnung an den Rolls Royce "Twenty" wurde dieses Kinderauto von der englischen Firma Triang 1930 hergestellt. Es wurde durch einen Elektromotor angetrieben. Türen und Motorhaube konnten geöffnet werden. Auf einer englischen Auktion wurde er für 700 Pfund zugeschlagen.

Questa vetturetta a pedali è una Chrysler della Steelcraft americana fabbricata verso il 1932: ha carrozzeria in lamiera, ruote cerchiate in gomma, trombetta e fanali funzionanti. La foto è del 1980: al volante c'è il piccolo Jason Peter Kelley accanto al padre Dale, direttore della rivista americana "Antique Toy World".

This pedal-car is a Chrysler, from the American Steelcraft, made around 1932. It has a metal body, wheels with rubber tyres, a horn and lights which actually work. The photo was taken in 1980: at the wheel is the young Jason Peter Kelley next to his father Dale, editor of the American magazine "Antique Toy World".

Cette voiture à pédales est une Chrysler du fabricant américain Steelcraft. Produite vers 1932, sa carrosserie est en tôle et les roues ont un bandage de caoutchouc; un klaxon à cornet et des lanternes fonctionnantes complètent l'ensemble. La photo date de 1980: au volant le petit Jason Peter Kelley à côté de son père Dale, directeur de la revue américaine "Antique Toy World".

Dieses von der amerikanischen Firma Steelcraft um 1932 hergestellte Tretauto stellt einen Chrysler dar: es hat eine Blechkarosserie, Räder mit Gummireifen, Hupe und funktionierende Scheinwerfer. Die Aufnahme stammt von 1980: am Steuer sitzt der kleine Jason Peter Kelley neben seinem Vater Dale, dem Direktor der amerikanischen Zeitschrift "Antique Toy World".

Questa imponente vettura sportiva per bambini porta la data del 1936 e venne fabbricata negli Stati Uniti. Era equipaggiata con un motore a scoppio capace di sviluppare una velocità di circa 50 km/h.

This impressive sports car for children carries the date 1936 and was made in the United States. It was equipped with a combustion engine and could get up to a speed of about 50 kmph.

Cette imposante auto de sport pour enfants porte la date de 1936. Fabriquée aux Etats Unis, elle était équipée d'un moteur à explosion qui la propulsait à 50 km/h.

Dieses eindrucksvolle Kindersportauto trägt die Jahreszahl 1936 und wurde in den Vereinigten Staaten hergestellt. Es war mit einem Verbrennungsmotor, der eine Höchstgeschwindigkeit von 50 km/std. erzielen konnte, ausgerüstet.

Mano nella mano due giovanissimi automobilisti del 1938: il maschietto è a bordo di una Peugeot a pedali, la bambina guida una vetturetta della Eureka francese.

Two young motorists hand in hand in 1938: the little boy is in a pedal Peugeot, and the girl is driving a French car from Eureka.

Deux jeunes automobilistes la main dans la main en 1938: le petit garçon est à bord d'une Peugeot à pédales et sa compagne conduit une Euréka française.

Hand in Hand zwei blutjunge Autofahrer von 1938: der Junge sitzt am Steuer eines Tret-Peugeots, das Mädchen lenkt ein Wägelchen der französischen Firma Eureka.

Stati Uniti 1932: una bella vetturetta a pedali che porta il nome Lincoln e la targa Pioneer. La carrozzeria è in robusta lamiera, le ruote in gomma.

United States 1932: a fine pedal-car which carries the name Lincoln and the license plate Pioneer. The body is made of strong metal and the wheels of rubber.

Etats Unis, 1932: une belle auto à pédales portant la marque Lincoln et la plaque Pioneer. La carrosserie est en tôle épaisse et les roues ont un bandage en caoutchouc.

Vereinigte Staaten 1932: ein schönes Tretauto mit dem Namen Lincoln und dem Schild Pioneer. Die Karosserie ist aus kräftigem Eisenblech, die Räder sind gummibereift.

Questa eccellente riproduzione della Hispano Suiza "six", costruita dai Signori Conduche e Pascal, fu presentata a Montlhéry nel 1933. Aveva un motore di 100 cc, velocità di 50 km/h., serbatoio di 3 litri.

This excellent reproduction of the Hispano Suiza "six" built by Conduche and Pascal, was presented at Montlhéry in 1933. It had a 100 cc. engine, could do 50 kmph. and a petrol tank with a 3 litre capacity.

Cette excellente reproduction de l'Hispano Suiza "six" réalisée par Messieurs Conduche et Pascal fut présentée à Montlhéry en 1933. Son moteur de 100 cm³ alimenté par un réservoir de 3 l. lui permettait une vitesse de 50 km/h.

Diese ausgezeichnete Reproduktiòn des Hispano Suiza "six", hergestellt von den Herren Conduche und Pascal, wurde in Montlhery 1933 vorgestellt. Das Rennautochen hatte einen Motor von 100 ccm, erzielte eine Höchstgeschwindigkeit von 50 km/std., der Tank faßte 3 Liter.

Ancora un modello anni trenta che riprende il classico stile Bugatti. Questa vetturetta a pedali fu presentata in una vendita all'asta della Casa Sotheby nel 1978.

Another thirties model which takes on the classic Bugatti style. This pedal-car was offered at auction at Sothebys in 1978.

Encore un modèle des années trente qui reprend le style classique de Bugatti. Cette voiture à pédales a été présentée à une vente aux enchères de Sotheby en 1978.

Noch ein Modell der Dreißigerjahre, das sich am klassischen Bugatti-Stil inspiriert. Dieses Pedalautochen wurde bei einer Auktion des englisches Hauses Sotheby 1978 angeboten.

1934: quasi una vettura vera questo raffinato cabriolet per bambini conosciuto come "Elve" e prodotto in Inghilterra dalla Welhams Renault Sales di Surbiton. Era provvisto di motore elettrico, fari, pneumatici, cofano e sportelli apribili.

1934: this sophisticated convertible for children, known as "Elve", was almost a real car. Made in England by Welhams Renault Sales of Surbiton, it was provided with an electric motor, lights, tyres, and a bonnet and doors which could be opened.

1934: presque une véritable voiture que ce cabriolet raffiné pour enfants connu comme "Elve" et produit en Grande Bretagne par Welhams Renault Sales de Surbiton. Elle était équipée d'un moteur électrique, de phares et de pneus; les portières et le coffre s'ouvraient.

1934: dieses unter dem Namen "Elve" bekannte und in England von der Firma Welhams Renault Sales von Surbiton hergestellte raffinierte Kinder-Kabriolett ist fast ein echtes Auto. Es verfügte über einen Elektromotor, Scheinwerfer, Gummireifen; Kühlerhaube und Türen konnten geöffnet werden.

Questa elegante vetturetta a pedali, riproduce in versione sportiva la Panhard "6CS" 6 cilindri di proprietà del Sultano del Marocco; al volante c'è suo figlio, Principe Moulay Hassan, che la ebbe in dono dalla Casa francese nel 1934.

This elegant pedal-car is a sports version of the Panhard "6CS" 6 cylinder owned by the Sultan of Marocco; at the wheel is his son, Prince Moulay Hassan to whom it was given by the French firm in 1934.

Cette élégante auto à pédales reproduit en édition sportive la Panhard "6CS" 6 cylindres de Sultan du Maroc. Au volant le prince Moulay Hassan, son fils, qui la reçu di constructeur français en 1934.

Dieses elegante Tretwägelchen gibt die Sportausführung des Panhard "6CS" mit Sechszylindermotor, das im Besitz des Sultans von Marokko ist wieder. Am Steuer sitzt sein Sohn, Prinz Moulay Hassan, der das Autochen von der französischen Fabrik 1934 aks Geschenk erhalten hatte.

Un'altra Renault "Elve", prodotta nel 1934 in Inghilterra dalla Welhams Renault Sales. Era un magnifico cabriolet a due posti, con luci, capottina ripiegabile e pneumatici.

Another Renault, known as "Elve", made in England in 1934 by Welhams Renault Sales. It was a magnificent two seater convertible with lights, a convertible roof and tyres.

Une autre Renault connue sous le nom de "Elve" et produite en Grande Bretagne en 1934 par Welhams Renault Sales. C'était un magnifique cabriolet deux places avec phares, pneus et capote rabattable.

Ein weiterer als "Elve" bekannter, 1934 in England von der Firma Welhams Renault Sales hergestellter Renault. Es war ein herrliches zweisitziges Kabriolett mit Scheinwerfern, Faltverdeck und Gummireifen.

Catalogo francese anni trenta con una ricca gamma di auto a pedali. Vi figurano auto della Eureka, modelli Renault e Peugeot. In basso appare una indovinata riproduzione della "Petite Rosalie" che costava allora 225 franchi; a fianco un modello di lusso Panhard dal rispettabile prezzo di 750 franchi.

A French catalogue of the thirties with a wide range of pedal-cars. Cars from Eureka, Peugeot and Renault models, are featured. At the bottom is a successful reproduction of the "Petite Rosalie" which cost at the time 225 francs; beside it is a de luxe Panhard model which cost the considerable sum of 750 francs.

Catalogue français des années trente avec une gamme étoffée d'autos à pédales: Euréka, modèles Renault et Peugeot. En bas, une reproduction réussie de la "Petite Rosalie" qui coûtait alors 225 francs; à côté, un modèle de luxe Panhard au prix respectable de 750 francs.

Französischer Katalog der Dreißigerjahre mit einer großen Auswahl an Tretautos. Hier sind Autos der Firma Eureka, sowie Renault- und Peugeotmodelle aufgeführt. Unten kann man eine gelungene Nachbildung der "Petite Rosalie" erkennen, die damals 225 Franken kostete; daneben ein Luxusmodell Panhard zum stattlichen Preis von 750 Franken.

1935: un giovanissimo partecipante alla famosa corsa Londra-Brighton a bordo di una divertente riproduzione di un autobus londinese a pedali. Il suo nome era Ernest Johnstone.

1935: a very young participant in the famous London to Brighton race on board a charming pedal reproduction of a London bus. His name was Ernest Johnstone.

1935: un tout jeune participant à la célèbre course Londres-Brighton à bord d'une amusante reproduction d'un autobus londonien à pédales. Son nom: Ernest Johnstone.

1935: ein blutjunger Teilnehmer an dem berühmten Rennen London - Brighton am Lenkrad einer amüsanten Nachbildung eines Londoner Autobusses mit Pedalantrieb. Er hieß Ernest Johnstone.

Riley madre e figlia in una foto del 1936: la imponente 2 litri 6 cilindri di Freddie Dixon, dopo la vittoriosa stagione sportiva, posa accanto ad una graziosa copia della stessa vettura.

The Rileys, mother and daughter in a photo of 1936: the impressive 2 litre 6 cylinder car of Freddie Dixon, after the victorious sports season, is shown next to a delightful copy of it.

Riley mère et fille sur une photo de 1936: l'imposante 2 litres six cylindres de Freddie Dixon après sa saison sportive victorieuse pose à côté d'une gracieuse copie pour juniors.

Riley, Mutter und Tocher auf einer Aufnahme von 1936: der stattliche Sechszylinder-Zweiliter-Rennwagen von Freddie Dixon, steht nach einer siegreichen Saison neben einer anmutigen Kopie seiner selbst.

Anni trenta: con il suo bravo casco da corsa questo giovane pilota conduce una piccola Amilcar durante una gara per bambini. Si noti la trasmissione a cinghia laterale.

The thirties: with his fine crash helmet this young driver is driving a small Amilcar in a race for children. Note the side driving belt.

Années trente: casqué comme il se doit, ce jeune pilote conduit une petite Amilcar dans une course pour enfants. On remarque la transmission par courroie latérale.

Dreißigerjahre: mit seinem flotten Sturzhelm lenkt dieser junge Rennfahrer seinen kleinen Amilcar durch das Kinderrennen. Zu beachten ist der seitliche Riemenantrieb.

EDW. K. TRYON COMPANY, PHILADELPHIA

AUTOMOBILES — BABY WALKABOUT — PEDAL BIKE

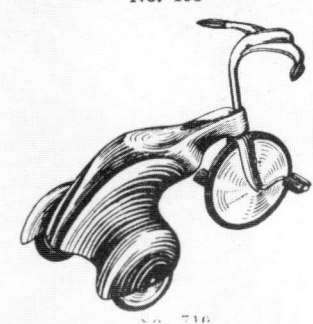

No. 125—Skippy Graham. 53 inches long overall. Maroon and cream finish. Adjustable rubber pedals. 9½-inch wheels, ¾-inch rubber tires. Electric horn (less battery). One in crate, set up, 65 lbs.
Each $19.50

No. 117—Skippy Roadster. 45 inches long overall. Die-formed body, streamlined. Brown and cream finish. High speed ball bearing gear revolving in lubricant within sealed housing unit. Adjustable rubber pedals. 9½-inch wheels, ⅝-inch rubber tires. Non-electric headlights. Electric horn (less batteries). One in carton, set up, 62 lbs. Each $15.95

No. 113—Buick. Body and fenders in one. 39½ inches overall. Cream with red finish. Adjustable rubber pedals. 8-inch wheels, ⅝-inch rubber tires. Non-electric headlights. Electric horn, less batteries. One in carton, set up, 39 lbs. Each $12.25

No. 107—Pontiac. Body and fenders in one. 36 inches long overall. Red with aluminum finish. Adjustable pedals. 8-inch wheels, ½-inch rubber tires. Non-electric headlights. One in carton, set up, 36 lbs.
Each $9.25

No. 103—Terraplane. 35 inches long overall. Green and cream finish. Adjustable pedals. 8-inch wheels, ½-inch tires. Non-electric headlights. One in carton, K. D., 29 lbs. Each $7.50

No. 157—Fire Chief. Body and fenders in one. 39½ inches long overall. Red and white finish. Adjustable rubber pedals. 8-inch wheels, ⅝-inch rubber tires. Electric headlights, less batteries. Fire siren. Fire bell. One in carton, set up, 38 lbs.
Each $11.95

No. 153—Fire Chief. 35 inches long overall. White and red finish. Adjustable rubber pedals. 8-inch wheels, ½-inch rubber tires. Nickeled fire bell. Non-electric headlights. One in carton, K. D., 29 lbs.
Each $8.25

No. 173—Fire Patrol. 47 inches long overall. Red and white finish. Adjustable pedals. 8-inch wheels, ⅝-inch rubber tires. Nickeled fire bell. 2 ladders. One in carton, 50 lbs. Each $14.50

No. 171—Fire Patrol. 43 inches long overall. Red and white finish. Adjustable pedals. 8-inch wheels, ½-inch rubber tires. Nickeled fire bell. 2 ladders. One in carton, K. D., 45 lbs. Each $12.50

No. 193—Speed Truck. 48 inches long overall. Green and cream finish. Adjustable rubber pedals. 8-inch wheels, ⅝-inch rubber tires. End gate opens when box is raised, closes when lowered. One in carton, K. D., 50 lbs. Each $12.25

No. 191—Dump Truck. 45 inches long overall. Cream and red finish. Adjustable rubber pedals. 8-inch wheels, ½-inch tires. Automatic end gate. One in carton, K. D., 39 lbs. Each $9.50

No. 855—Baby Walkabout. 24¼ inches long overall. Seat height, 9 inches. 18 inches wide overall. 4½-inch rear wheels, ½-inch tires; front wheel, 2¾ x ½ inch rubber composition. 3 in carton, K. D., 43 lbs. Each $4.50

No. 710—Streamlined Pedal Bike. 22 inches long overall. Seat height, 10¼ inches. Red and cream finish. Front wheel, 8-inch; rear, 5-inch, ½-inch rubber tires. Block rubber pedals. One-piece body. 6 in carton, 60 lbs. Each $1.60

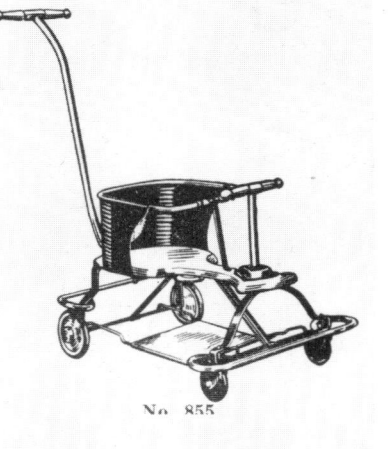

1938: un catalogo americano della Edw. K. Tryon di Philadelphia. Vi compaiono diverse auto a pedali con il caratteristico "musone" a spartivento che andava di moda in quegli anni.

1938: an American catalogue from Edw. K. Tryon of Philadelphia. Other pedal-cars with it have the characteristic wind divider "nose" which was fashionable in those years.

1938: un catalogue américain de Edw. K. Tryon de Philadelphie. On y découvre plusieurs autos à pédales au "museau" fendant l'air comme le voulait la mode de l'époque.

1938: ein amerikanischer Katalog der Firma Edw. K. Tryon aus Philadelphia. Hier sind eine ganze Reihe von Tretautos mit der typischen, in jenen Jahren modernen windschnittigen "Schnauze" zu sehen.

Ancora un modello anteguerra della Triang inglese: un piccolo camioncino a due posti in lamiera, che venne messo in commercio nel 1939.

Another pre-war model from the English Triang: a small model two seater lorry which was put on the market in 1939.

Encore un modèle Triang anglais d'avant la guerre: un petit camion deux places en tôle lancé sur le marché en 1939.

Noch ein Vorkriegsmodell der englischen Firma Triang: ein kleiner zweisitziger Blechlastwagen, der 1939 in den Handel kam.

Classico modello anni trenta questo spider per bambini: azionato a pedali, disponeva di fari elettrici, tromba, ruote cerchiate in gomma. La carrozzeria, bicolore, era in robusta lamiera.

This spider for children was a classic thirties model: it was operated by pedals, and had electric lights, a horn, and rubber rimmed wheels. The two-coloured body was made of strong metal.

Modèle classique des années trente, ce spider à pédales était équipé de lanternes électriques, d'un klaxon et de roues à bandage en caoutchouc. La carrosserie, bicolore, était en tôle épaisse.

Ein klassisches Modell der Dreißigerjahre ist dieser Kinder-Spider: durch Pedale angetrieben, verfügte er über elektrische Scheinwerfer, Hupe, gummibereifte Räder, eine zweifarbige Karosserie aus kräftigem Blech.

Le auto a pedali in legno erano molto comuni in Italia prima della guerra: questo modello piuttosto bizzarro e con qualche pretesa aerodinamica è degli ultimi anni trenta.

Wooden pedal-cars were very common in Italy before the war: this rather strange model, with some aerodynamic pretences is from the late thirties.

Les autos à pédales en bois étaient très répandues avant la guerre en Italie. Ce modèle plutôt bizarre et avec quelques prétentions aérodynamiques, remonte à la fin des années trente.

Tretautos aus Holz waren vor dem Krieg in Italien sehr verbreitet: dieses eher wunderliche Modell mit einem gewissen Anspruch auf Windschnittigkeit stammt vom Ende der Dreißigerjahre.

Un'altra vetturetta in legno piuttosto semplice: fu prodotta in Italia poco prima della guerra. Di fianco la stessa vetturetta in una cartolina del 1940.

Another fairly simple wooden model: it was produced in Italy shortly before the war. By the side is the same car on a postcard of 1940.

Une autre auto en bois assez simple produite en Italie peu avant la deuxième guerre mondiale. A côté, la même voiture sur une carte postale de 1940.

Ein weiteres eher einfaches Holzkinderauto, das in Italien kurz vor dem Krieg hergestellt wurde. Daneben dasselbe Autochen auf einer Postkarte von 1940.

A destra: "Bimbo Racer V. 12": questa vetturetta a due posti, che arieggiava uno spider Ferrari degli anni cinquanta, venne fabbricata in Italia nel 1956 dalla Sila in alcune migliaia di esemplari. Motore elettrico, pneumatici in gomma, carrozzeria in fibra di vetro, luci, claxon, velocità 7-8 km/h, lunghezza m. 1,70.

To the right: "Bimbo Racer V. 12": this two-seater model, which copied a Ferrari spider of the 50s, was made by the Italian firm Sila in 1956. Thousands of models were made, and it had an electric motor, rubber wheels, a fibreglass body, lights, a hooter, went at 7-8 kmph. and was 1.70 metres long.

A droite: "Bimbo Racer V. 12": cette petite auto deux places qui évoquait un spider Ferrari années cinquante, a été fabriquée en Italie à partir de 1956 par la firme Sila à quelques milliers d'exemplaires. Moteur électrique, pneus en gomme, carrosserie en fibre de verre, feux, klaxon; vitesse 7-8 km/h, longueur 1,70 m.

Rechts: "Bimbo Racer V.12": dieser kleine Zweisitzer, der einen Ferrari Spider der Fünfzigerjahre nachahmt, wurde in Italien 1956 von der Sila in einigen Tausenden von Exemplaren produziert. Elektromotor, Gummireifen, Fiberglaskarosserie, Scheinwerfer, Hupe, Höchstgeschwindigkeit 7-8 km/std., Länge 1,70 m.

Sogni proibiti davanti ad una vetrina natalizia allestita a Londra prima della guerra. Fanno bella mostra alcuni piccoli capolavori della Triang, tra cui la Vauxhall 1932 al centro.

Forbidden dreams in front of a shop window in London decked out for Christmas before the war. The fine display is made up by some small masterpieces from Triang, among which the Vauxhall of 1932 in the centre.

Rêves inaccessibles devant une vitrine de Noël à Londres avant la guerre. On peut y admirer quelques petits chefs-d'œuvre de Triang, entre autres la Vauxhall 1932 au centre.

Verbotene Träume vor einem Weihnachtsschaufenster in London vor dem Krieg. Im Mittelpunkt stehen einige kleine Meisterwerke der Firma Triang, unter ihnen, in der Mitte, ein Vauxhall von 1932.

Stati Uniti, 1938: una vetturetta a pedali che arieggia lo stile automobilistico del tempo. Al volante è James L. Goulding Jr., oggi collezionista di giocattoli.

United States 1938: a pedal-car which imitates the style of motorcars of the time. At the wheel is Mr. James L. Goulding Jr., now a collector of toys.

Etats Unis, 1938: une auto à pédales au goût automobile de l'époque. Au volant, James L. Goulding Jr., aujourd'hui collectionneur de jouets.

Vereinigte Staaten 1938: ein Tretauto, das den Stil der damaligen Automobile nachahmt. Am Steuer sitzt James L. Goulding Jr., heute Spielzeugsammler.

Ancora una vetturetta a pedali della Triang inglese apparsa alla fine degli anni cinquanta. La linea ricorda quella della Vanwall Grand Prix 1957.

Another pedal-car from the English company Triang which appeared at the end of the fifties. The shape recalls that of the Vanwall Grand Prix 1957.

Encore une auto à pédales du constructeur anglais Triang apparue à la fin des années cinquante. Sa ligne rappelle celle de la Vanwall Grand Prix 1957.

Noch ein Tretauto der englischen Firma Triang, das Ende der Fünfzigerjahre auf den Markt kam. Die Linie erinnert an die des Vanwall Grand Prix von 1957.

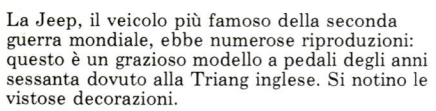

La Jeep, il veicolo più famoso della seconda guerra mondiale, ebbe numerose riproduzioni: questo è un grazioso modello a pedali degli anni sessanta dovuto alla Triang inglese. Si notino le vistose decorazioni.

Numerous reproductions of the Jeep, the most famous vehicle of the second world war, were made: this is a delightful pedal model of the sixties produced by Triang. Please note the striking decorations.

La Jeep, le véhicule le plus célèbre de la deuxième guerre mondiale a été maintes fois reproduit. Ici, il s'agit d'un sympathique modèle à pédales des années soixante produit par Triang. On remarque les décorations voyantes.

Der Jeep; das berühmteste Fahrzeug des 2. Weltkriegs, erlebte viele Nachbildungen: dies hier ist ein anmutiges Tretmodell der Sechzigerjahre der englischen Firma Triang. Beachtenswert sind die auffälligen Verzierungen.

Le auto per bambini si aggiornano continuamente: questa vetturetta a pedali di produzione italiana è ispirata ai bolidi di Formula 1 degli anni sessanta.

Cars for children are constantly being brought up to date: this Italian produced pedal model was inspired by the Formula 1 racing cars of the sixties.

Les autos pour enfants évoluent constamment: ce modèle de production italienne s'inspire des bolides de Formule 1 des années soixante.

Kinderautos passen sich ständig der Mode an: dieses Tretauto italienischer Produktion inspiriert sich an den Formel 1 Rennwagen der Sechzingerjahre.

Mini Alfa Disneyland: uno slanciato spider per bambini costruito nel 1968 dalla fabbrica italiana Ceada: aveva motore elettrico, freni a comando meccanico, carrozzeria in vetroresina, claxon, luci. Velocità 15 km/h, lunghezza m. 2,10.

Mini Alfa Disneyland: a streamlined spider for children built by the Italian factory Ceada in 1968; it had an electric motor, mechanically controlled brakes, fibreglass body, hooter and lights. Speed 15 kmph, length 2.10 metres.

Mini Alfa Disneyland: un spider élancé pour enfants,; réalisé en 1968 par le constructeur italien Ceadas. Moteur électrique, freins à commande mécanique, carrosserie en résine de verre, klaxon, feux. Vitesse 15 km/h, longueur 2,10 m.

Mini Alfa Disneyland: ein schlanker Spider für Kinder, 1968 von der italienischen Fabrik Ceada hergestellt: er besaß einen Elektromotor, mechanisch bedienbare Bremsen, Glasfaserkunststoffkarosserie, Scheinwerfer, Hupe; Höchstgeschwindigkeit 15 km/std., Länge 2,10 m.

1968: questa è la Mini-Lotus fabbricata in Italia dalla Canni-Ferrari. Aveva un motore a scoppio di 98 cc, telaio tubolare, sterzo a cremagliera, freni a disco, velocità regolabile da 15 a 50 km/h.

1968: this is the Mini-Lotus made in Italy by Canni-Ferrari. It had a 98 cc. combustion engine, a tubular chassis, a rack steering wheel, disc brakes and a speed variable from 15 to 50 kmph.

1968: voici la Mini-Lotus fabriquée en Italie par Canni-Ferrari. Moteur à explosion de 98 cm^3, châssis tubulaire, direction à crémaillère, freins à disque, vitesse de 15 à 50 km/h.

1968: dies ist der Mini-Lotus, in Italien von der Firma Canni-Ferrari hergestellt. Er besaß einen Verbrennungsmotor von 98 ccm Hubraum, einen Rohrrahmen, eine Zahnstangenlenkung, Scheibenbremsen, eine von 15 bis 50 km/std. einstellbare Geschwindigkeit.

Un pezzo unico che riproduce l'Alfa Romeo "RL" Targa Florio e fu realizzato anni addietro dalla Carrozzeria Riva.

A one-off model which reproduces the Alfa Romeo "RL" Targa Florio. It was built years before by the Riva coachmakers.

Ce modèle unique reproduisant l'Alfa Romeo "RL" Targa Florio fut réalisé il y a des années par la Carrosserie Riva.

Eine Einzelstück, das den Alfa Romeo "RL" Targa Florio wiedergibt. Vor einigen Jahren wurde es von der Karosseriewerkstatt Riva gebaut.

Una graziosa vetturetta per bambini che riproduce fedelmente la Ford "T" 1910. Tra gli altri particolari si noti la bella capottina in tela ripiegabile. Era prodotta dalla Somec italiana.

A delightful car for children which faithfully reproduces the Ford "T" 1910. Among the other details, note the nice cloth top that can be folded back. It was made by the Italian Somec.

Une sympathique auto, reproduisant fidèlement la Ford "T" 1910. Entre autres détails, on remarque la belle capote rabattable en toile. Elle était produite par Somec Italiana.

Ein anmutiges Kinderauto, das getreu den Ford "T" von 1910 wiedergibt. Unter den weiteren technischen Einzelheiten ist das schöne Faltverdeck aus Leinwand erwähnenswert. Es wurde von der italienischen Firma Somec hergestellt.

L'interesse per le auto d'epoca arriva anche alle vetturette per bambini: negli anni sessanta la Somec italiana produce repliche in miniatura di auto da museo. Questa è ispirata ad una Rambler d'inizio secolo.

The interest in old cars began to effect cars for children; in the sixties the Italian Somec was producing miniature replicas of cars in museums for toy shops. This one was inspired by a Rambler from the beginning of this century.

La passion pour les voitures d'époque touche aussi les autos pour enfants: au cours des années soixante, Somec Italiana produit des répliques miniatures des autos de musée. Celleci s'inspire d'une Rambler du début du siècle.

Das Interesse für die Oldtimer greift auch auf die Kinderautos über: in den Sechzigerjahren produziert die italienische Firma Somec Miniatur-Nachbildungen von Museumsstücken. Das gezeigte Modell inspiert sich an einem Rambler vom Beginn unseres Jahrhunderts.

Le tradizioni automobilistiche di Torino, patria della Fiat, si ritrovano anche fra le auto per bambini: al Parco del Valentino dal lontano 1929 i bambini possono noleggiare delle vetturette a pedali, ormai divenute famose. Generazioni di torinesi hanno pedalato su queste vetture, sempre del medesimo proprietario.

The motoring traditions of Turin, home of Fiat, are evident too in cars for children. As long ago as 1929 children could hire the famous pedalcars in the Parco del Valentino. Generations of people from Turin have pedalled in these cars which are still owned by the same person.

La tradition automobile de Turin, patrie de Fiat, se retrouve aussi dans les autos pour enfants: au Parc du Valentino dès 1929, les enfants peuvent louer des autos à pédales désormais célèbres. Des générations de turinois ont pédalé dans ces voitures, toujours appartenues au même propriétaire.

Die Automobiltradition von Turin, der Heimat des Fiats, findet sich auch beim Kinderauto wieder: seit 1929 können die Kinder im Valentino-Park nunmehr schon berühmt gewordene Tretautos mieten. Ganze Generationen von Turinern sind in diesen Wägelchen, die ihren Besitzer seither nicht gewechselt haben, munter tretend gefahren.

In alto: Italia, 1969; una divertente riproduzione della vettura alata apparsa nel film "Chitty Chitty Bang Bang" della italiana Pines. Accanto, l'auto di Topolino realizzata dalla Giordani.

Top, Italy 1969: an amusing reproduction of the winged car from the film "Chitty Chitty Bang Bang", made by Pines. At the side, Micky Mouse's car, built by Giordani.

En haut: Italie, 1969. Une amusante reproduction de la voiture ailée du film "Chitty Chitty Bang Bang", fabriquée en 1969 par la firme italienne Pines. A côté, l'auto de Mickey réalisée par Giordani.

Oben: Italien 1969; eine amüsante, von der italienischen Firma Pines ausgeführte Nachbildung des geflügelten Wagens, der im Film "Chitty Chitty Bang Bang" zu sehen war. Daneben das von der Firma Giordani hergestellte Auto von Mickymaus.

Nel 1968 la fabbrica italiana Ampaglass mise in commercio una serie di vetturette a pedali con il padiglione staccabile, riproducenti auto del tempo. Questa era la Mini-Fiat 500.

In 1968 the Italian company Ampaglass put on the market a series of pedal-cars with detachable hoods which reproduced certain motorcars of the time. This was the Mini-Fiat 500.

En 1968, la maison italienne Ampaglass lança une série d'autos à pédales avec pavillon amovible, qui reproduisaient les voitures de l'époque. Celle-ci est une Mini-Fiat 500.

1968 brachte die italienische Firma Ampaglass eine Reihe von Tretautos mit abnehmbarem Dachaufbau in den Handel, die den damaligen Automobilen nachgebildet waren. Dies hier ist ein Mini-Fiat 500.

Una coppia di vetturette a pedali con carrozzeria in plastica fabbricate in Italia nel 1968: a sinistra una riproduzione della "Spring", a destra una Volkswagen "Maggiolino". Erano entrambe della Pines.

Two pedal-cars with plastic bodies produced in Italy in 1968. On the left is a reproduction of the "Spring", on the right a Volkswagen "Maggiolino". They were both from Pines.

Deux autos à pédales avec carrosserie en plastique fabriquées en Italie en 1968; à gauche une reproduction de la "Spring", à droite une Volkswagen "Coccinelle". Toutes deux étaient produites par Pines.

Ein paar Tretautos mit Plastikkarosserie, in Italien 1968 hergestellt: links eine Reproduktion des "Spring", rechts ein Volkswagen "Käfer". Beide stammen von der Firma Pines.

Mini Chaparral "2F": una delle tre spettacolose vetturette della Mini-Champs di Henri Barthel. È provvista di motore a scoppio, freni a disco ed è lunga m. 2,65.

Mini Chaparral "2F": one of the three spectacular Mini-Champs cars by Henri Barthel. It is provided with a combustion engine, disc brakes and is 2.65 metres long.

Mini-Chaparral "2F": une des trois autos spectaculaires de la Mini-Champs d'Henri Barthel. Elle est équipée d'un moteur à explosion et de freins à disque; longueur 2,65 m.

Mini Chaparral "2F": eines der beeindruckendsten Modelle der Firma Mini-Champs von Henri Barthel. Es ist mit einem Verbrennungsmotor und Scheibenbremsen ausgestattet und ist 2,65m lang.

93

Lo starter ha da poco dato il via ad una gara per bambini in cui sono impegnate alcune vetturette con motore a scoppio della Mini-Champs riproducenti la famosa Ferrari "330 P2".

The starter has just given the signal for this children's race: taking part are some Mini-Champs model cars with combustion engines which copy the famous Ferrari "330 P2".

Le départ vient d'être donné à cette course pour enfants; on y voit quelques autos équipées d'un moteur à explosion de la Mini-Champs reproduisant la fameuse Ferrari "330 P2".

Der Starter hat soeben das Startzeichen für ein Kinderrennen gegeben, an dem einige Kinderautos mit Verbrenungsmotor der Firma Mini-Champs teilnehmen, die den berühmten Ferrari "330 P2" nachbilden.

Un famoso modello a pedali costruito dalla Austin Junior Car Factory: la "J40" nota anche come "Joy Car". Questa bella vetturetta venne prodotta dal 1949 al 1971 in ben 32.000 esemplari.

A famous pedal model constructed by the Austin Junior Car Factory: the "J40" also called the "Joy Car". This fine small car was produced from 1949 to 1971, during which time a good 32,000 models were made.

Un célèbre modèle à pédales fabriqué par Austin Junior Car Factory: la "J40", connue aussi comme "Joy Car". Cette belle petite auto a été produite à 32.000 exemplaires de 1949 à 1971.

Ein berühmtes, von der Austin Junior Car Factory gebautes Tretmodell: der auch unter dem Namen "Joy Car" bekannte "J40". Dieses schöne Wägelchen wurde von 1949 bis 1971 in mehr als 32.000 Exemplaren hergestellt.

Una pagina pubblicitaria italiana degli anni ottanta in cui è stata utilizzata, per reclamizzare dei biscotti, una vetturetta Austin "J40".

An Italian advertisement from the eighties in which an Austin "J40" model car is used to advertise biscuits.

Une annonce publicitaire italienne des années quatre-vingts où l'on a utilisé une Austin "J40" pour réclamiser une marque de biscuits.

Eine italienischen Werbeanzeige der Achtzigerjahre, in der für eine Keks-Reklame ein Kinderauto Austin "J40" verwendet wurde.

Italia, 1949: per qualche tempo le fabbriche riproponevano modelli apparsi prima della guerra. Questa è una Giordani che era in catalogo già una quindicina d'anni prima.

Italy 1949: for some time factories went on promoting models which had appeared before the war. This is a Giordani which had appeared in a catalogue fifteen years earlier.

Italie, 1949: pendant quelques temps encore, les constructeurs proposèrent de modèles apparus avant la guerre. Voici une Giordani qui était au catalogue une quinzaine d'années auparavant.

Italien 1949: einige Zeit lang boten die Hersteller Vorkriegsmodelle an. Hier wird ein Giordani gezeigt, der schon 15 Jahre zuvor in einem Katalog aufgeführt war.

Una delle ultime auto vecchia maniera prodotte in questo dopoguerra: un piccolo spider con carrozzeria in lamiera e le caratteristiche ruote a raggi con pneumatici in gomma.

One of the last cars for children in the old style produced in this post war period: a small spider with a metal body and the characteristic spoked wheels with rubber tyres.

Une des dernières autos pour enfants vieille manière produites dans d'après-guerre: un petit spider avec une carrosserie en tôle et les caractéristiques roues à rayons avec bandages en caoutchouc.

Eines der letzten Kinderautos im alten Stil, der in der Nachkriegszeit hergestellt wurde: ein kleiner Spider mit Blechkarosserie und den typischen gummibereiften Speichenrädern.

To Thrill Young Drivers — the Finest on Wheels

A. STATION WAGON. A real beauty ... the pride-and-joy of its young driver! Steers with ease, turns in small circles. Tail gate may be raised and lowered. Box section is large, gives plenty of sitting or carrying space. Fine steel body boasts gleaming, maroon enamel finish. Solid rubber tires, ball-bearing wheels. Horn. 47 inches long. (38) $20.95

B. POLICE CAR. Gleaming white car is all a boy could ask for! With siren, spotlight (batteries not furnished), adjustable radio aerial. Rubber tires, adjustable pedals. Finest workmanship ... of heavy steel. Over-all length, 33 inches. (30) $13.95

C. FIRE CHIEF CAR. Give him this streamlined, "Kidillac" beauty ... the finest you can choose. 1950 design, low for extra driving ease. Of one-piece steel, without a seam or joint. Fire bell with chain, thick rubber tires. Fireman's red finish. (31) $23.50

D. FIRE TRUCK. The most beautiful fire truck a child could find under the tree! Newly designed model: full ball bearing wheels and driving mechanism, finer steering, undergear. Hand rails, rear deck and rear step afford standing position or seat for second child. Rubber tires. Strong wooden ladders are removable. With loud bell. Heavy steel body, finished bright red. (40) $20.95

Un esempio dello stile delle auto a pedali del dopoguerra: questo è un catalogo americano del 1950. Hanno ancora carrozzerie in metallo, ma l'era della plastica è ormai vicina.

An example of the post-war style of pedal-car: this is an American catalogue of 1950. They still have metal bodies but the age of plastic was getting near.

Un exemple du style des autos à pédales de l'après-guerre: un catalogue américain de 1950. Leurs carrosseries sont encore métalliques, mais l'ère du plastique est désormais aux portes.

Ein Beispiel für den Stil der Tretautos der Nachkriegszeit: hier ein amerikanischer Katalog von 1950. Die Wäglechen weisen noch Metallkarosserien auf, doch ist das Kunststoff-Zeitalter nunmehr schon nahe.

Italia, 1949: il costruttore Piero Patria lancia una singolare vetturetta per bambini denominata "Lucciola". Aveva tre ruote gommate, motore elettrico, fari, claxon e freni ad espansione. Velocità 10 km/h., lunghezza m. 1,70. A destra due pagine del catalogo 1952, dove si vede la "Lucciola" impegnata in diverse manifestazioni.

Italy 1949: the manufacturer Piero Patria launches a very special car for children called the "Lucciola". It had three wheels with tyres, un electric motor, headlamps, a horn and expansion brakes. Speed 10 kmph, length 1.70 m. On the right, two pages from the 1952 catalogue, showing the "Lucciola" taking part in various events.

Italie, 1949: le constructeur Piero Patria lance une singulière voiture pour enfants baptisée "Lucciola". Elle avait trois roues à bandage de caoutchouc, un moteur électrique, des phares, un klaxon et des freins à expansion. Vitesse 10 km/h, longueur 1,70 m. A droite, deux pages du catalogue 1952 où l'on voit la "Lucciola" engagé dans diverses manifestations.

Italien 1949: der Konstrukteur Piero Patria bringt ein originelles, "Lucciola" (Glühwürmchen) genanntes Kinderauto heraus. Es besaß drei Gummiräder, einen Elektromotor, Scheinwerfer, Hupe und Innenbackenbremsen. Höchstgeschwindigkeit 10 km/std., Länge 1,70 m. Rechts zwei Seiten des Katalogs von 1952, auf denen das "Glühwürmchen" bei verschiedenen Veranstaltungen gezeigt wird.

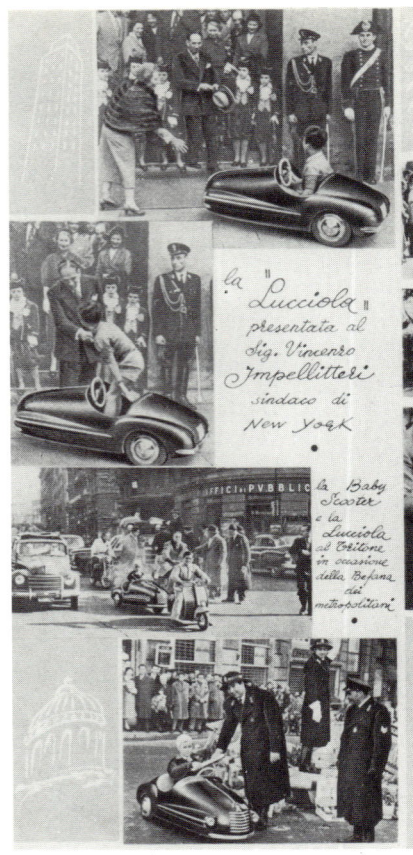

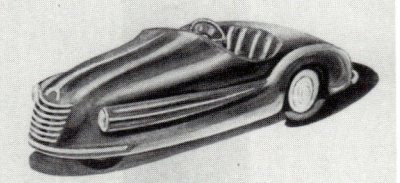

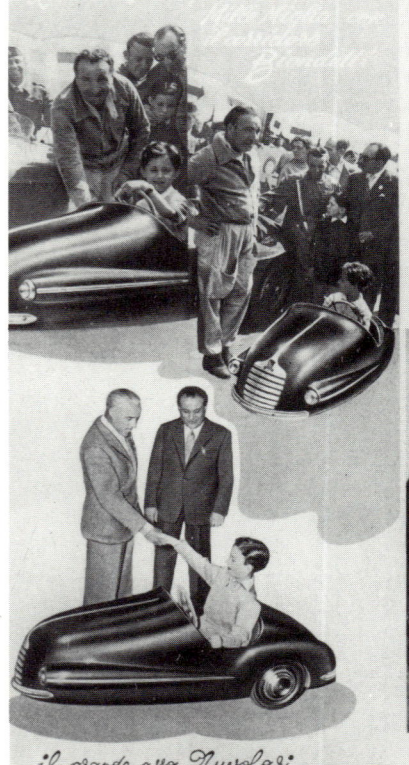

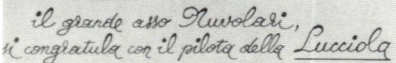

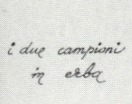

98

Ancora la "Lucciola" di Piero Patria. In alto, Torino, Stadio Comunale: prima del Derby Juventus-Torino il piccolo Franco Patria con l'amico De Petrini compie il giro d'onore sulla pista attorno al campo a bordo della "Lucciola". Sotto, il piccolo Franco Patria intervistato da un giornalista.

Piero Patria's "Lucciola" again. Above: the Stadio Comunale at Turin. Before the start of the Derby Juventus-Torino, little Franco Patria with his friend De Petrini, in his "Lucciola" does the lap of honour on the track round the field. Below: Franco Patria being interviewed by a journalist.

Encore la "Lucciola" de Piero Patria. En haut, Turin, Stade Municipal: avant le derby Juventus-Torino, le petit Franco Patria et son ami De Petrini effectuent un tour d'honneur de la piste entourant le terrain à bord de la "Lucciola". Dessous: le petit Franco Patria interviewé par un journaliste.

Noch einmal das "Glühwürmchen" von Piero Patria. Oben, Turin, Städtisches Stadion: vor dem Fußball-Lokalderby Juventus-Torino fährt der kleine Franco Patria mit seinem Freund De Petrini die Ehrenrunde am Steuer des "Glühwürmchen" auf der Rundbahn, die das Fußballfeld ainschließt. Unten, der kleine Franco Patria wird von einem Journalisten interviewt.

Lancia "D.50" Formula 1 del 1954-55: esemplare unico costruito per il figlio del corridore Alberto Ascari e ritrovato da Francis Mortarini. Lunga m. 1,90, peso 90 kg, questa Lancia in miniatura aveva un motore a scoppio di 40 cc posteriore e poteva viaggiare ad oltre 30 km/h. Il cruscotto disponeva di cronometro e contachilometri.

Lancia "D.50" Formula 1, 1954-55: a unique example built for the son of the racing driver Alberto Ascari, and rediscovered by Francis Mortarini. This miniature Lancia was 1.90 metres long and weighed 90 kg. It had a 49 cc. combustion engine at the rear and could travel at more than 30 kmph. The dashboard had a chronometer and a speedometer.

Lancia "D. 50" Formule 1, 1954-55: exemplaire unique réalisé pour le fils du pilote Alberto Ascari et retrouvé par Francis Mortarini. D'une longueur de 1,90 m pour un poids de 90 kg, cette Lancia en miniature était équipée d'un moteur à explosion de 49 cm^3 monté à l'arrière qui lui permettait de dépasser 30 km/h. Un chronomètre et un compteur kilométrique complétaient la planche de bord.

Lancia "D. 50", Formel 1 1954-55: einziges, für den Sohn des Rennfahrers Alberto Ascari gebautes Exemplar, das Francis Mortarini aufgespürt hat. Länge 1,90 m, Gewicht 90 kg; dieser Miniatur-Lancia besaß einen Verbrennungsheckmotor von 49 ccm und erzielte eine Reisegeschwindigkeit von über 30 km/std. Auf dem Amaturenbrett befanden sich eine Stoppuhr und ein Kilometerzähler.

AUTO SPORT GRAN LUSSO

Caractéristiques générales du type « LUSSO » mais phares et sonnette fonctionnent parmi de batterie — Modern disque aux roues de ⌀ mm 140 — Pneus blancs de ⌀ mm 25 — cm 96 x 30 x 40 poid Kg. 9.

Il peut être fourni, sur demande, avec carillon et antenne.

CAMIONCINO

Elegant modèle de conception moderne pour enfants de 2 à 6 ans — Carrosserie en tôle d'acier — Siège réglable — Tableau de bord avec horloge et compte-kilomètres — Parabrise démontable — Coffre avec finisages chromés — Roues mm 130 — Pneus mm 15 — Petit caisson arrière avec trappe de décharge — Mouvement à pédale — Long. cm. 96 — Large. cm. 40.

AUTO GRAND PRIX

Tipo lusso — Caratteristiche del tipo normale in più: Claxon — Paraurti con guarnizione — Anelli gomma bianca ballonicno da mm. 25 — Cappellotti grandi alle ruote — Dimensioni cm. 110 x 45.

Per bambini da 3 a 7 anni.

AUTO CORSA Indianapolis ELETTRICA — GIORDANI

1. Motore - alimentazione a corrente continua - alla tensione di 12 Volta potenza HP. 1/10" a 6000 giri
2. Reostato - per regolazione velocità
3. Invertitore di marcia (cambio) con posizione di folle
4. Batteria a 12 Volta - misura d'ingombro cm. 24 x 45,5 x 17,5 con valvola automatica di sicurezza
5. Acceleratore regolabile
 * La spostabilità dell'acceleratore consente di adattare l'auto all'uso di qualsiasi bambino dell'età da 3 a 9 anni.
6. Velocità regolabile - massima Km. 8 h
7. Autonomia Km. 25-30
8. Peso senza batteria Kg. 25 circa
9. Pendenza superabile del 8-10%

Dimensioni: lunghezza cm. 130 larghezza cm. 63 - altezza cm. 46.

Accessori a richiesta: Piccolo raddrizzatore di corrente a 3 amp/h per ricarica batteria - voltaggio a richiesta.

IMPORTANTE: Movimenti montati su boccole di materiale antifrizione. La speciale sistemazione della pedaliera consente l'uso della vettura a bambini da 3 a 9 anni.

Le attrezzature elettriche sono state studiate e vengono costruite dalla Ditta Domo S.p.A. - Bologna.

AUTO CORSA Indianapolis ELETTRICA — GIORDANI

Pagine stralciate da cataloghi Giordani del dopoguerra: le vetturette illustrate sono rispettivamente degli anni 1951, 1952 e 1957.

A page taken from a Giordani post-war catalogue; the models illustrated are, respectively, from 1951, 1952 and 1957.

Pages tirées de catalogues Giordani d'après-guerre: les modèles illustrés sont de 1951, 1952 et 1957 respectivement.

Aus Giordani-Katalogen der Nachkriegszeit gelöste Seiten: die dargestellten Kinderautos stammen jeweils aus den Jahren 1951, 1952 und 1957.

Francia 1954: concorso di eleganza per vetture da bambini. In primo piano una monoposto e uno spider a due posti che recano sul cofano il nome Calox.

France 1954: an "elegance" competition for children's cars. In the front, a single seater car and a two seater spider which bears the name Calox on the bonnet.

France, 1954: concours d'élégance pour autos d'enfants. Au premier plan une monoplace et un spider deux places avec la marque Calox sur le coffre.

Frankreich 1954: Eleganzwettbewerb für Kinderautos: im Vordergrund ein Einsitzer und ein Spider Zweisitzer, die auf der Kühlerhaube den Namen Calox tragen.

USA, 1955: un industriale californiano costruì a Lawndale una apposita pista dove i bambini potevano provare le emozioni di un autodromo. Ecco una "bagarre" in miniatura poco dopo il via.

USA 1955: a Californian industrialist built at Lawndale a special track where children could experience the emotion of a real race track. Here is a "bagarre" in miniature soon after the start.

USA, 1955: un industriel californien fit construire à Lawndale une piste où les enfants pouvaient éprouver les émotions de la course. Voici une "bagarre" en miniature peu après le départ.

USA 1955: ein kalifornischer Industrieller ließ in Lawndale extra eine Rennbahn errichten, auf der die Kinder die Erregung eines Autodroms auskosten konnten. Hier sehen wir eine Miniatur-"Bagarre" kurz nach dem Start.

Gara di vetturette "midget" per bambini a Lawndale negli Stati Uniti: un concorrente con tanto di casco posa per i fotografi prima del via.

A competition for "midgets" for children in Laundale, U.S.A.: a competitor with a rather large helmet poses for a photograph before the start.

Course de "Midget" pour enfants à Lawndale aux Etats Unis: un concurrent dûment casqué pose pour les photographes avant le départ.

Ein Rennen von Kinderrennautos "midget" in Lawndale in den Vereinigten Staaten: ein kleiner Teilnehmer mit seinem Sturzhelm stellt sich vor dem Start den Fotografen.

Una vetturetta vecchio stampo prodotta negli anni sessanta in Italia dalla Somec: riproduce la famosa Itala 1907 del raid Pechino-Parigi. Un raid che, fatto a colpi di pedali, sarebbe un po' duro.

A model car in the old style produced in the sixties by Somec in Italy: it reproduces the famous Itala 1907 of the Pecking to Paris race. A race which would be pretty hard to pedal.

Une voiturette vieille école réalisée par la Somec en Italie dans les années soixante: elle reproduit la célèbre Itala 1907 du raid Paris-Pékin. Un raid plutôt dur à coups de pédales.

Ein von der Firma Somec in Italien in den Sechzigerjahren hergestelltes Kinderauto vom alten Schlag: es gibt den berühmten Itala von 1907 wieder, der die Streiffahrt Peking-Paris bestritten hatte. Ein änliches Unternehmen wäre für die kleinen Pedalritter wohl zu hart.

Dall'album di famiglia. Prima foto: il piccolo Carlo su una vetturetta di legno, Italia 1949. Seconda: Franco nel 1961 al Parco del Valentino di Torino. Terza: romantico bacio di Marina all'automobilista in erba, Italia 1955. Quarta: una vetturetta Giordani stile Studebaker nel 1960. Quinta: Jean Louis nel 1949 con la sua Jeep.

From a family album. First photo: young Carlo in a wooden model car, Italy 1949. Second: Franco in 1961 in the Parco del Valentino in Turin. Third: a romantic kiss from Marina to the learner driver, Italy 1955. Fourth: a Giordani model car in the style of Studebaker in 1960. Fifth: Jean Louis in 1949 with his Jeep.

Tiré de l'album de famille. Première photo: le petit Carlo dans une auto en bois, Italie 1949; deuxième: Franco en 1961 au parc du Valentino de Turin; troisième: un baiser romantique de Marina au pilote en herbe, Italie 1955; quatrième: une auto junior Giordani style Studebaker en 1960; cinquième: Jean Louis en 1949 avec sa Jeep.

Aus dem Familienalbum. Erstes Foto: der kleine Carlo in einem Holzautochen, Italien 1949. Zweites Foto: Franco 1961 im Valentino-Park von Turin. Drittes Foto: Romantischer Kuß Marinas für den kleinen Autofahrer im Grase, Italien 1955. Viertes Foto: ein Kinderauto Giordani im Stil Studebaker im Jahre 1960. Fünftes Foto: Jean-Louis mit seinem Jeep, 1949.

Perfetta riproduzione della famosa Land Rover realizzata nel 1962 in Inghilterra per l'erede del re di Giordania. Al volante della vetturetta, provvista di motore, luci e sportelli apribili, è il figlio di Mr. Wilks, direttore tecnico della Rover. A destra: la "Mini Jeep" costruita nel 1969 in Italia dalla Italtoy. Motore di 42 cc, velocità 16 km/h.

A perfect reproduction of the famous Land Rover built in England in 1962 for the heir of the of Jordan. At the wheel of the model car is the son of Mr Wilks, the technical director of Rover. Below, the "Mini Jeep" built in Italy in 1969 by Italtoy. 42 cc motor, speed 16 kmph.

Parfaite reproduction de la célèbre Land Rover réalisée en 1962 en Grande Bretagne pour l'héritier au trône jordanien. Au volant de la Jeep, le fils de M. Wilks directeur technique de Rover.
A droite, la "Mini Jeep" réalisée en Italie par Italtoy en 1969. Moteur de 42 cm³, vitesse de 16 km/h.

Vollkommene Reproduktion des berühmten Land Rover, die 1962 in England für den Thronfolger des Königs von Jordanien verwirklicht wurde. Am Steuer des Wägelchens sitzt der Sohn des technischen Direktors der Roverwerke Mr. Wilks. Rechts: der 1969 in Italien von der Firma Italtoy hergestellte "Mini Jeep". Motor von 42 ccm Hubraum, Höchstgeschwindigkeit 16 km/std.

Sull'onda del successo dei film di James Bond "Agente segreto 007" venne costruita in Inghilterra questa perfetta riproduzione della famosa Aston Martin "DB5" donata per il Natale del 1966 al figlio dello Scià. Al volante è il figlio del Direttore della Aston Martin.

Following the success of the James Bond "Secret Agent 007" films, this perfect reproduction of the famous Aston Martin "DB5" was made in England and given to the son of the Shah for Christmas 1966. At the wheel is the son of the managing director of Aston Martin.

Dans la foulée des films de James Bond agent secret 007, on réalisa en Grande Bretagne cette parfaite reproduction de la fameuse Aston Martin "DB5" donnée à Noël 1966 au fils du Shah. Au volant, le fils du directeur d'Aston Martin.

Im Kielwasser des Erfolges der der James-Bond-Filme "Geheimagent 007" wurde in England diese perfekte Nachbildung des berühmten Aston Martin "DB5" gebaut, als Weihnachtsgeschenk für den Sohn des Schahs (1966). Am Steuer sitzt der Sohn des Direktors der Aston Martin.

In Inghilterra negli anni sessanta venne messa sul mercato questa interessante automobile per bambini chiamata "Cheetah Cub Car", che riproduceva la linea della Jaguar "D". Tra le altre caratteristiche disponeva di motore a scoppio di 75 cc, luci, claxon e carrozzeria in fibra di vetro.

In England in the sixties this interesting car for children called the "Cheetah Cub Car" was put on the market. It recalled the lines of the Jaguar "D" and among the other characteristic had a 75 cc. combustion engine, lights, a hooter and a fibreglass body.

C'est en Grande Bretagne dans les années soixante que fut lancée cette intéressante auto junior baptisée "Cheetah Cub Car", qui reproduisait la ligne de la Jaguar "D". Entre autres caractéristiques, elle possédait un moteur à explosion de 75 cm³, des phares, un klaxon et une carrosserie en fibre de verre.

Im England der Sechzigerjahre wurde dieses interessante Kinderauto mit Namen "Cheetah Cub Car" auf den Markt gebracht, das die Linie des Jaguar "D" nachahmte. Unter den weiteren Kennzeichen: Verbrennungsmotor von 75 ccm Hubraum, Scheinwerfer, Hupe und Glasfiberkarosserie.

La strepitosa Mini Ferrari "330 P2" costruita nel 1956 da Francis Mortarini per la Scaf di Parigi. Motore a due tempi di 72 cc, velocità 25/40 km/h, carrozzeria in fibra di vetro, ruote imitazione Dunlop, freni a tamburo, fari anteriori e posteriori, châssis tubolare, lunghezza m. 2,50, peso 100 kg.

The striking Mini Ferrari "330 P2" built in 1956 by Francis Mortarini for Scaf of Paris. It had a two-stroke 72 cc. engine which did a speed of 25 to 40 kmph., a fibreglass body, imitation Dunlop wheels, drum brakes, front and back lights, a tubular chassis and was 2.50 metres long and weighed 100 kg.

La fantastique Mini Ferrari "330 P2" réalisée en 1962 par Francis Mortarini pour la Scaf de Paris. Moteur deux temps de 72 cm^3, vitesse 25/40 km/h, carrosserie en fibre de verre, roues imitation Dunlop, freins à tambour, feux avants et arrières, châssis tubulaire, longueur 2,50 m, poids 100 kg.

Der phantastische Mini Ferrari "330 P2", 1956 von Francis Mortarini für die Firma Scaf aus Paris gebaut. Zweitaktomotor von 72 ccm Hubraum, Geschwindigkeit 25/40 km/std., Glasfiberkarosserie, Scheinwerfer und Rückleuchten, Rohrrahmen, Länge 2,50 m, Gewicht 100 kg.

1972: lezioni di guida a sei anni d'età. L'iniziativa era dell'inglese Mike Hugues, proprietario di una autorimessa a Beaconsfield, che intendeva preparare i futuri automobilisti con queste vetturette capaci di viaggiare a circa 30 km/h.

1972: driving lessons at six years old. This idea was started up by an Englishman, Mike Hugues, a garage owner of Beaconsfield, who intended to prepare future drivers in this way with these cars which could travel at about 30 kmph.

1972: auto-école à six ans. L'initiative fut prise par l'anglais Mike Hughes, propriétaire d'un garage à Beaconsfield, qui voulait ainsi préparer les futurs automobilistes avec ces autos en mesure de rouler à 30 km/h.

1972: Fahrschule mit sechs Jahren. Diese Initiative ging von dem Engländer Mike Hugues aus, dem Besitzer einer Autoreparaturwerkstatt in Beaconsfield, der die zukünftigen Autofahrer mit diesen Auto, die eine Höchstgeschwindigkeit von ungefähr 30 km/std. erzielen konnten, auf den Straßenverkehr vorbereiten wollte.

1966: partenza della "24 Minuti" di Le Mans. In questa gara riservata alle auto per bambini e disputata sul circuito della Sarthe, furono protagoniste le vetturette di Francis Mortarini di cui si vedono alcune Mini Ferrari "330 P2" e Ford Mini "GT 40" allineate davanti ai box.

1966: the start of the "24 Minutes" at Le Mans. In this race reserved for children's cars and contested on the Sarthe circuit, the miniature cars of Francis Mortarini took part. We see here some Mini Ferrari "330 P2"s and Ford Mini "GT 40" lined up in front of the garages.

1966: départ de la "24 Minutes du Mans". Dans cette course réservée aux autos juniors et disputée sur le circuit de la Sarthe, les autos de Francis Mortarini se taillèrent la part du lion; on voit quelques Mini Ferrari "330 P2" et Ford Mini "GT 40" alignées devant les boxes.

1966: Start der "24 Minuten" von Le Mans. In diesem den Kinderautos vorbehaltenen Rennen, das auf dem Ring der Sarthe ausgetragen wurde, spielten die Mini-Autos von Francis Mortarini, von dem einige Mini Ferrari "330 P2" und Ford Mini "GT 40" vor den Boxen aufgereiht zu sehen sind, eine bedeutende Rolle.

Ford Mini "GT 40" della Scaf: la seconda spettacolosa vetturetta per bambini costruita da Francis Mortarini e uscita per il Salone dell'Automobile di Parigi del 1966. Le caratteristiche tecniche erano pressappoco le stesse della Mini Ferrari, ma il posto guida poteva essere anche al coperto.

A Ford Mini "GT 40" from Scaf: the second spectacular model car for children built by Francis Mortarini came out for the Salon de l'Automobile in Paris in 1966. The technical characteristics were practically the same as in the Mini Ferrari but the driving seat could also be covered.

Ford Mini "GT 40" de la Scaf: la deuxième auto junior réalisée par Francis Mortarini et présentée au Salon de l'Automobile de Paris en 1966. Les caractéristiques techniques étaient à peu de choses près les mêmes que celles de la Mini Ferrari, mais le poste de pilotage pouvait aussi être fermé.

Der Ford Mini "GT 40" der Firma Scaf: das zweite großartige Kinderauto, das Francis Mortarini baute und das 1966 auf dem Automobilsalon von Paris herauskam. Die technischen Kennzeichen waren ungefähr die gleichen wie die des Mini Ferrari, der Fahrersitz konnte aber auch mit einem Verdeck geschlossen werden.

109

Una superba riproduzione della Matra F.1 per ragazzi di oltre 13 anni che volevano seguire la scuola di pre-pilotaggio sportivo.
La produsse in pochi esemplari nel 1967 la Scaf di Mortarini. Motore di 100 cc, velocità 70 km/h, lunghezza m. 2,98.

A superb reproduction of the Matra F. 1 for children of 13 and over who wanted to attend the school for sporting young racing drivers. Mortarini's Scaf produced a few models in 1967. It had 100 cc. engine, did 70 kmph., and was 2.98 metres long.

Une superbe reproduction de la Matra de F. 1 pour enfants de plus de 13 ans désireux de suivre l'école de pré-pilotage sportif. Produite en quelques exemplaires seulement par la Scaf de Mortarini, ce modèle était équipé d'un moteur de 100 cm³ lui permettant d'atteindre une vitesse de 70 km/h, pour une longueur de 2,98 m.

Eine außergewöhnliche Nachbildung des Matra F. I für Jungen über 13 Jahre, die eine Vor-Fahrschule für Sportfahrer besuchen wollten. Er wurde 1967 in wenigen Exemplaren von der Firma Scaf Mortarinis hergestellt. Motor von 100 ccm Hubraum, Höchstgeschwindigkeit 70 km/std., Länge 2,98 m.

Italia 1979: esce la "Ferrarina" che riproduce la "312 T2" Formula 1 di Niki Lauda. Monta un motore a scoppio di 60 cc e può raggiungere i 60 km/h. Ha cambio a due marce più retromarcia, freni a disco, avviamento elettrico, cerchioni in lega, pneumatici Tubeless "slick", scocca in vetroresina, cintura di sicurezza. Peso 100 kg, lunghezza m. 2,40. Oggi è presentata dalla Motor Pony.

Italy 1979: the "Ferrarina" which reproduced Niki Lauda's "312 T2" Formula 1 came out. It had a 60 cc. combustion engine and could get up to 60 kmph. It has two gears plus a reverse gear, disc brakes, an electric starter, alloy wheel rims, Tubeless "slick" tyres, a fibreglass body and safety belts. Weight 100 kg., length 2.40 metres. Today it is available from Motor Pony.

Italie, 1979: apparition de la "Ferrarina" reproduisant la "312 T2" Formule 1 de Niki Lauda. Equipée d'un moteur à explosion de 60 cm³, elle peut atteindre 60 km/h. L'équipement comprend: boîte à deux vitesses plus marche arrière, freins à disque, démarrage électrique, jantes en alliage léger, pneus Tubeless "slick", coque un résine de verre, ceintures de sécurité. Poids 100 kg, longueur 2,40 m. Elle est présentée par la Motor Pony.

Italien 1979: es kommt der "Ferrarina" auf den Markt, der den Formel 1 Rennwagen "312 T2" von Niki Lauda in klein wiedergibt. Er besitzt einen Verbrennungsmotor von 60ccm Hubraum und erreicht eine Spitzengeschwindigkeit von 60km/st. Er ist mit einem Zweiganggetriebe mit Rückwärtsgang, Scheibenbremsen, elektrischem Anlasser, Leichtmetallfelgen, schlauchlosen Reifen "slick", Karosserie in Fiberglas, Sicherheitsgurten ausgerüstet. Gewicht 100kg, Länge 2,40m. Heute wird er von der Motor Pony angeboten.

Star 55: questa vetturetta fabbricata in Francia nel 1979 dalla Arola riproduce la Bugatti "55" Super Sport 1932. È lunga 2 metri, ha un motore a scoppio Sachs di 47 cc. carrozzeria in vetroresina, luci, velocità 40 km/h.

Star 55; this car made in France in 1979 by Arola reproduces the Bugatti "55" Super Sport 1932. It is 2 metres long, has a Sachs 47 cc. combustion engine, a glass fibre body, lights and can do 40 kmph.

Star 55: cette petite auto réalisée en France en 1979 par Arola reproduit la Bugatti "55" Super Sport 1932. Longueur 2 m, moteur à explosion Sachs de 47 cm³, carrosserie en résine de verre, feux, vitesse 40 km/h.

Star 55: dieses 1979 in Frankreich von der Firma Arola hergestellte Kinderauto gibt den Bugatti "55" Super Sport von 1932 wieder. Es ist 2m lang, hat einen Sachs-Verbrennungsmotor von 47 ccm Hubraum, eine Karosserie in Fiberglas, Beleuchtung, Höchstgeschwindikkeit 40 km/std.

Una indovinata riproduzione del furgoncino Citroën "5 CV" degli anni venti dovuto alla fabbrica inglese Lely Small Cars. Funziona a pedali, dispone di luci elettriche e ha la portiera posteriore apribile.

A clever reproduction of the small Citroën "5 CV" van of the twenties, coming from the English factory, Lely Small Cars. It is operated by pedals, has electric lights and the back door can be opened.

Une reproduction très réussie du fourgon Citroën "5 CV" des années vingt, du constructeur anglais Lely Small Cars. Elle fonctionne à pédales et son équipement comprend les feux électriques et la malle arrière ouvrante.

Eine gelungene Reproduktion des Lieferwagens Citroën "5 CV" der Zwanzigerjahre, von der englischen Fabrik Lely Small Cars hergestellt. Sie verfügt über einen Pedalantrieb, elektrische Scheinwerfer; die Ladeklappe kann geöffnet werden.

Una Citroën dei nostri giorni: la "2 CV 6" prodotta nel 1982 dalla inglese Lely Small Cars. Al volante è la piccola Polly Lely, figlia del costruttore.

A present-day Citroën: the "2 CV 6" produced in 1982 by the English Lely Small Cars. At the wheel is young Polly Lely, the maker's daughter.

Une Citroën actuelle: la "2 CV 6" produite en 1982 par la firme anglaise Lely Small Cars. Au volant, la petite Polly Lely fille du constructeur.

Ein Citroën unserer Tage: der "2 CV 6", 1982 von der englischen Firma Lely Small Cars produziert. Am Steuer die kleine Polly Lely, die Tochter des Konstrukteurs.

La Panda ha avuto una pronta risposta fra le auto per bambini: questa vetturetta, costruita in versione a pedali ed elettrica, è opera della italiana Nuova Sogimez.

The Panda quickly found a place among children's cars: this model, in pedal and electric versions, is made by the Italian firm Nuova Sogimez.

La Panda, d'emblée a inspiré les constructeurs d'autos pour enfants. Cet exemplaire, réalisé en version à pédales et électrique, est de la firme italienne Nuova Sogimez.

Der Panda, hat auf dem Kinderautomarkt sofort ein Echo gefungen: Dieses mit Pedalen und elektrischem Antrieb lieferbare Modell stammt von der italienischen Firma Nuova Sogimez.

Sono di moda le Formula 1 Grand Prix: la italiana Gagliardi monta su un telaio standard tre carrozzerie diverse in vetroresina riproducenti bolidi di Formula 1. Il motore è un Morini di 50 cc potenziato, il cambio a due marce più retromarcia, i freni a disco. Lunghezza m. 2,20.

Formula 1 Grand Prix models are the fashion: the Italian Gagliardi uses a standard chassis for three different glass fibre bodies each representing a Formula 1 racing car. The motor is a 50 cc. Morini, it has two gears plus a reverse, and disc brakes. The length is 2.20 metres.

Les Formule 1 Grand Prix sont à la mode: le constructeur italien Gagliardi monte, sur un châssis standard, trois carrosseries différentes en résine de verre reproduisant des bolides de F. 1. Le moteur Morini de 50 cm³ est élaboré et l'équipement comprend une boîte à deux rapports plus marche arrière et des freins à disque. La longueur est de 2,20 m.

Die Formel 1 Grand Prix Renwagen sind modern: die italienische Firma Gagliardi montiert auf ein Standardfahrgestell drei verschiedene Fiberglaskarosserien, die die Formel 1 Rennwagen nachbilden. Der Motor ist ein Morini von 50 ccm Hubraum, hochfrisiert, Zweigangschaltung mit Rückwärtsgang, Scheibenbremse, Länge 2,20 m.

La Morgan "4/4", una delle più prestigiose vetture inglesi, in una bella riproduzione a pedali dovuta alla Hamilton Brooks & Co. Ha telaio metallico, carrozzeria in fibra di vetro, lunghezza m. 1,25.

The Morgan "4/4", one of the most prestigious of English cars, in a fine pedal version made by Hamilton Brooks & Co. It has a metal chassis, glass fibre body and is 1.25 metres long.

La Morgan "4/4", une des plus prestigieuses voitures anglaises dans une reproduction de la Hamilton Brooks & Co. Châssis métallique, carrosserie en fibre de verre, longueur 1,25 m.

Der Morgan "4/4", eines der bedeutendsten englischen Autos, in einer schönen Tretausführung, die von der Firma Hamilton Brooks & Co. gebaut wurde. Er hat einen Metallrahmen, eine Karosserie in Fiberglas und ist 1,25 m lang.

Aria di nostalgia anche fra le auto a pedali: questa bella riproduzione della Citroen "5CV" anni venti è fabbricata oggi in Inghilterra dalla Lely Small Cars. La vetturetta è lunga m. 1,37, dispone di luci ed è costruita a mano.

Air of nostalgia even among pedal-cars: this fine reproduction of the Citroën "5 CV" of the twenties is today made in England by Lely Small Cars. The car is 1.37 metres long, has lights and is built by hand.

Atmosphère nostalgique pour les autos à pédales aussi: cette belle reproduction de la Citroën "5 CV" années vingt est fabriquée aujourd'hui en Grande Bretagne par Lely Small Cars. Réalisée à la main, la voiture est équipée de feux. Longueur 1,37 m.

Nostalgiewelle auch bei den Tretautos: diese schöne Reproduktion des Citroën "5CV" der Zwanzigerjahre wird heute in England von der Lely Small Cars hergestellt. Das Autochen ist 1,37 m lang, verfügt über eine Beleuchtungsanlage und ist handgefertigt.

La Mercedes "540 K" Baby scala 1:2 del costruttore svizzero Franco Sbarro. È una delle più spettacolose vetture per bambini dei nostri giorni. Ha un motore di 47 cc, telaio tubolare, cambio a due velocità, avviamento elettrico, sospensioni indipendenti, pneumatici, carrozzeria in poliestere. Trasporta due passeggeri alla velocità di 45 km/h. Il cruscotto è completo di strumentazione, l'interno finemente impellicciato. Dispone di luci anteriori e posteriori. Peso 90 kg, lunghezza m. 2,65.

The Mercedes "540 K" Baby on a scale of 1:2 from the Swiss constructor Franco Sbarro. It is one of today's most spectacular cars for children. It has a 47 cc. engine, a tubular chassis, two gears, an electric starter, independent suspension, tyres, and a polyesterene body. It can carry two passengers at a speed of 45 kmph. The dashboard is covered with various instruments and the interior upholstered with fur. It has front and back lights. Weight 90 kg, length 2.65 metres.

La Mercedes "540 K" Baby à l'échelle 1:2 du constructeur suisse Franco Sbarro. il s'agit d'une des autos pour enfants les plus spectaculaires de notre époque. L'équipement comprend: moteur de 47 cm^3, châssis tubulaire, boîte à deux rapports, allumage électrique, suspensions indépendantes, pneus, carrosserie en polyester. Elle transporte deux passagers à la vitesse de 45 km/h. La planche de bord comporte une instrumentation complète. L'intérieur est habillé de façon raffinée. Poids 90 kg, longueur 2,65 m.

Der Mercedes "540 K" Baby, Maßstab 1:2, des schweizerischen Konstrukteurs Franco Sbarro. Er ist einer der auffälligsten Kinderautos unserer Tage. Er besitzt einen Motor von 47 ccm Hubraum, einen Rohrrahmen, Zweigangschaltung, elektrischen Anlasser, Einzelaufhängung, Gummireifen, Polyesterkarosserie, transportiert zwei Fahrgäste mit einer Geschwindigkeit von 45 km/st. Das Armaturenbrett ist mit Instrumenten komplett ausgestattet, das Innere ist fein ausgekleidet. Er verfügt über Scheinwerfer und Rückleuchten. Gewicht 90 kg, Länge 2,65 m.

Sbarro "Testa Rossa": una eccezionale replica della celebre Ferrari anni cinquanta. Adatta per ragazzi di circa 15 anni, è una vettura in piena regola con motore a scoppio di 15 cv., quattro marce più retromarcia, sospensioni sulle quattro ruote, freni a disco, avviamento elettrico, luci, carrozzeria monoscocca in vetroresina. Può viaggiare a 90 km/h, pesa 300 kg, lunghezza m. 3,30.

Sbarro's "Testa Rossa": an exceptional reproduction of the celebrated Ferrari of the fifties. Suitable for children of about 15 years old, it is a car in the real sense of the word, with a 15 hp combustion engine, four forward gears plus a reverse gear, four wheel suspension, disc brakes, electric starter, lights and a glass fibre monocoque body. It can travel at 90 kmph. It weighs 300 kg, and is 3.30 metres long.

Sbarro "Testa Rossa": une réplique exceptionnelle de la célèbre Ferrari années cinquante. Adaptée pour des enfants de 15 ans environ, il s'agit d'une voiture dans le vrai sens du mot. L'équipement comprend: moteur à explosion de 15 CV, boîte à quatre rapports plus marche arrière, suspensions sur les quatre roues, freins à disque, allumage électrique, feux, carrosserie monocoque en résine de verre. Elle atteint 90 km/h, pèse 300 kg pour une longueur de 3,30 m.

Sbarro "Rotkopf" (Testa Rossa): eine außergewöhnliche Nachbildung des berühmten Ferrari der Fünfzigerjahre. Geeignet für Jungen von ungefähr 15 Jahren, ist es ein voll funktionierendes Auto mit Verbrennungsmotor von 15 PS, Viergangschaltung und Rückwärtsgang, Federung an allen vier Rädern, Scheibenbremsen, elektrischem Anlasser, Beleuchtung, Glasfaserkunststoffkarosserie in Schalenbauweise. Es erzielt eine Reisegeschwindigkeit von 90 km/std., wiegt 300 kg, ist 3,30 m lang.

Un gruppo di vetturette per bambini appartenute alla straordinaria collezione di Francis Mortarini, l'appassionato francese che negli anni sessanta riuscì a mettere assieme diversi pezzi di eccezionale interesse. Si notino, tra le altre, la Cisitalia Grand Prix di Piero Patria color argento; al centro le due piccole Citroën e una Hispano Suiza della famiglia Esders.

A group of cars for children which go to make up part of the extraordinary collection of Francis Mortarini, the French enthusiast who, in the sixties, managed to get together several models of exceptional interest. Note the silver coloured Cisitalia Grand Prix by Piero Patria, the two little Citroëns in the centre and a Hispano Suiza belonging to the Esders family.

Un groupe d'autos pour enfants qui faisaient partie de l'extraordinaire collection de Francis Mortarini, le collectionneur français qui dans les années soixante était parvenu à rassembler divers exemplaires exceptionnels. On remarque, entre autres, la Cisitalia Grand Prix couleur argent de Piero Patria, les deux petites Citroën au centre et une Hispano Suiza de la famille Esders.

Eine Gruppe von Kinderautos aus der außergewöhnlichen Sammlung von Francis Mortarini, dem französischen Kinderautofan, dem es in den Sechzigerjahren gelungen war, verschiedene Stücke von außergewöhnlichem Interesse zusammenzustellen. Unter anderen sind bemerkenswert: der Cisitalia Grand Prix von Piero Patria, silberfarben, in der Mitte die beiden kleinen Citroën und ein Hispano Suiza der Familie Esders.

Queste pittoresche auto a pedali, che si fregiano dei nomi di Mercedes 1923 e Rolls Royce 1926, appartengono al Museo Automobilistico Haris Testverek di Budapest.

These picturesque pedal cars which were adorned with the names of Mercedes 1923 and Rolls Royce 1926 belong to the Haris Testverek Car Museum in Budapest.

Ces pittoresques autos à pédales portent les noms de Mercedes 1923 et de Rolls Royce 1926. Elles appartiennens au Musée Automobile Haris Testverek de Budapest.

Diese malerischen Tretautos, die sich mit den Namen Mercedes 1923 und Rolls Royce 1926 schmücken, gehören dem Automobilmuseum Haris Testverek von Budapest.

Inghilterra 1971: Jo-Mo-Ro racing car. Questo il nome della spettacolosa vetturetta da corsa qui illustrata che ha tutte le carte in regola per essere considerata una vera auto di Formula 1.

England 1971: Jo-Mo-Ro racing car. That was the name of the spectacular model racing car illustrated here which had all the necessary features to be considered a real Formula 1 car.

Grande Bretagne, 1971: Jo-Mo-Ro racing car. C'est le nom de cette spectaculaire auto de course qui a toutes les cartes en règle pour être considérée une authentique Formule 1.

England 1971: Jo-Mo-Ro racing car, das ist der Name des hier dargestellten großartigen Rennwägelchens, dem nichts fehlt, um als ein echter Formel 1 Rennwagen angesehen werden zu können.

La Replica BMW "328" accanto alla versione "Baby" per bambini, entrambe costruite da Franco Sbarro. Lunga m. 1,85, la vetturetta ha un motore di 47 cc, freni a disco posteriori, avviamento elettrico, luci. La carrozzeria è in vetroresina monoscocca. Velocità 30 km/h, peso 55 kg.

The Replica BMW "328" next to the "Baby" version for children, both constructed by Franco Sbarro. The car was 1.85 metres long, had a 47 cc engine, rear disc brakes, an electric starter and lights. The body was made of monocoque fibreglass. Speed 30 kmph, weight 55 kg.

La réplique BMW "328" à côte de la version "Baby" pour enfants, réalisées toutes deux par Franco Sbarro. Longueur 1,85 m, moteur de 47 cm³, freins à disque à l'arrière, démarrage électrique, feux. La carrosserie est en résine de verre monocoque. Vitesse 30 km/h, poids 55 kg.

Die Kopie BMW "328" neben der "Baby"-Ausführung für Kinder, beide von Francis Sbarro gebaut. Bei einer Länge von 1,85 m besaß das Autochen einen Motor von 47 ccm Hubraum, Scheibenbremsen hinten, einen elektrischen Anlasser, Scheinwerfer. Die Karosserie ist in Schalenbauweise aus Glasfiber hergestellt. Höchstgeschwindigkeit 30 km/std., Gewicht 55 kg.

Negli anni del boom dei karts venne costruita in Inghilterra questa vetturetta denominata Mirage. Aveva un motore a scoppio di 144 cc e poteva toccare i 40 km/h. Carrozzeria in vetroresina, lunghezza m. 1,68.

In the years of the go-kart boom this model car, called Mirage, was built in England. It had a 144 cc combustion engine and could reach 40 kmph. It had a fibreglass body and was 1.68 metres long.

C'est à l'époque du boom du karting que fut réalisée en Grande Bretagne cette petite auto baptisée Mirage. Son moteur à explosion de 144 cm³ la propulsait à 40 km/h. Carrosserie en résine de verre de 1,68 m de long.

In den Jahren des Booms der karts wird in England dieses Mirage benannte Mini-Auto gebaut. Es besaß einen Verbrennungsmotor von 144 ccm Hubraum und erzielte eine Höchstgeschwindigkeit von 40 km/std. Karosserie in Fiberglas, Länge 1,68 m.

Da cataloghi italiani degli anni ottanta: da sinistra, in alto la Rolls Royce della Peg-Pines, la Ferrari F.1 della Giordani, il trattore Massey-Ferguson della Rolly Toys, la Golf cabriolet della Peg-Pines.

From Italian catalogues of the eighties: on the left at the top the Peg-Pines Rolls Royce, the Ferrari F.1 from Giordani, the Massey-Ferguson tractor from Rolly Toys and the Golf convertible from Peg-Pines.

Catalogues italiens des années quatre-vingts: à gauche en haut la Rolls Royce de Peg-Pines, la Ferrari F. 1 de Giordani, le tracteur Massey-Ferguson de Rolly Toys, les Golf cabriolet de Peg-Pines.

Aus italienischen Katalogen der Achtzigerjahre: von links, oben der Rolls Royce der Firma Peg-Pines, der Ferrari F. 1 der Firma Giordani, der Traktor Massey-Ferguson der Firma Rolly Toys, der Golf Kabriolett der Firma Peg-Pines.

Inghilterra, 1981: la Saudia Williams Formula 1 nella pregevole riproduzione della Hamilton Brooks & Company. Questa vetturetta monta un motore elettrico capace di sviluppare una velocità di circa 30 km/h, ha freni a disco e pneumatici tipo slick.

England 1981: the valuable Hamilton Brooks & Company reproduction of the Saudia Williams Formula 1. This model car has an electric motor capable of reaching a speed of about 30 kmph., has disc brakes and "slick" tyres.

Grande Bretagne, 1981: la Saudia Williams de Formule 1 dans la très belle reproduction de Hamilton Brooks & Company. Equipée d'un moteur électrique lui permettant une vitesse de 30 km/h, l'auto est eu outre équipée de freins à disque et de pneus type slick.

England 1981: der Saudia Williams Formel 1 in der schönen Ausführung der Hamilton Brooks & Company. Dieses Rennwägelchen ist mit einem Elektromotor ausgestattet, der eine Spitzengeschwindigkeit von 30 km/std. entwickeln kann, hat Scheibenbremsen und Reifen vom Typ slick.

Un'altra vetturetta prodotta ultimamente dalla Hamilton Brooks & Company: riproduce la Triumph "TR. 7". È a pedali, lunga m. 1,75, carrozzeria in fibra di vetro.

Another model car recently produced by Hamilton Brooks & Company. It is a reproduction of the Triumph "TR. 7", a pedal car 1.75 metres long with a fibreglass body.

Un autre modèle récent de Hamilton Brooks & Company reproduit la triumph "TR. 7". Modèle à pédales de 1,75 m de longueur avec carrosserie en fibre de verre.

Ein weiteres in jüngster Zeit von der Hamilton Brooks & Company hergestelltes Kinderauto: es bildet den Triumph "TR. 7" nach. Pedalantrieb, Länge 1,75 m, Karosserie in Fiberglas.

Da cataloghi italiani degli anni ottanta: una Rolls Royce Junior e una Bugatti Junior, entrambe prodotte dalla italiana Sogimez.

From Italian catalogues of the eighties: the Rolls Royce Junior and the Bugatti Junior both from the Italian Sogimez.

Catalogues italiens des années quatre-vingts: la Rolls Royce Junior de Sogimez et la Bugatti Junior de Sogimez.

Italien, Achtzigerjahre: ein Rolls Royce Junior und ein Bugatti Junior, beide von der italienischen Firma Sogimez hergestellt.

Una vetturetta dalla linea avveniristica: la monoposto Rima prodotta in Italia. Dispone di un motore a due tempi di 49 cc, variatore di velocità o cambio, scocca in vetroresina.

A car along futuristic lines: the one seater Rima made in Italy. It has a two-stroke 49 cc. engine, speed variator or gear box, and a fibreglass body.

Une voiture à la silhouette futuriste que cette monoplace Rima produite en Italie. Elle dispose d'un moteur de 49 cm³, d'un variateur de vitesse ou d'une boîte; la coque est en résine de verre.

Ein Kinderauto mit zukunftsweisender Linie: der Einsitzer Rima aus Italien. Er verfügt über einen Zweitaktmotor von 49 ccm Hubraum, ein Variomatikgetriebe oder eine Gangschaltung, Glasfaserkunststoffkarosserie.

La Jeep per bambini prodotta dalla italiana Sila. Motore elettrico, velocità 7-8 km/h, impianto illuminazione, carrozzeria monoscocca.

The Jeep for children made by the Italian company Sila. It has an electric motor, a speed of 7 to 8 kmph, a set of lights and a monocoque body.

La Jeep pour enfants, produite par la firme italienne Sila. Moteur électrique, vitesse 7/8 km/h, équipement lumineux, carrosserie monocoque.

Der von der italienischen Firma Sila produzierte Kinder-Jeep. Elektromotor, Geschwindigkeit 7/8 km/std., Lichtanlage, Karosserie in Schalenbauweise.

Un mini-Maggiolino Volkswagen prodotto artigianalmente in Inghilterra dalla Casa Kitz. È lungo m. 2,20 e monta un motore di 5 cv. Dispone di una ricca serie di "optionals", fra cui il radiotelefono e il mangianastri.

A mini-Maggiolino Volkswagen, hand made in England by Casa Kitz. It is 2.20 m long, and has a 5 hp engine. It has a wide range of optionals, including a radio telephone and a cassette recorder.

Une mini-Coccinelle Volkswagen fabriquée artisanalement en Grande Bretagne par la firme Kitz. D'une longueur de 2,20 m., elle est animée par un moteur de 5 CV. Les nombreux équipements en option comprennent un radiotéléphone et un lecteur de cassettes.

Ein handwerklich in England von der Firma Kitz hergestellter Volkswagen Käfer in Miniatur. 2,20 m lang besitzt er einen Motor von 5 PS. Er verfügt über eine lange Reiche von "Extras", darunter ein Funktelefon und einen Cassettenrecorder.

Dalla Francia questo moderno fuoristrada per ragazzi: lo produce la Arola con motore a scoppio di 49 cc. Velocità 20 km/h, carrozzeria in poliestere, equipaggiamento da vero fuoristrada.

This modern beach buggy comes from France: it is made by Arola, has a 49 cc. combustion engine and can travel at 20 kmph. The body is made of polyesterene and the car is equipped like the realthing.

Ce tout-terrain pour enfants vient de France où il est produit par Arola avec un moteur à explosion de 49 cm^3. Vitesse 20 km/h, carrosserie en polyester, équipement complet du véritable tout-terrain.

Aus Frankreich stammt dieser moderne Geländewagen für Kinder: die Firma Arola stellt ihn mit einem Verbrennungsmotor von 49 ccm Hubraum her. Höchstgeschwindigkeit 20 km/std., Polyesterkarosserie, Ausstattung eines echten Geländewagens.